T0247614

Museums and Heritage Tourism

This book examines the symbiotic relationship between museums, heritage attractions and tourism, using a range of international case studies.

Divided into three clear sections, the author first outlines a theoretical framework for understanding the role of museums in heritage tourism, before addressing the practical challenges of interpretation, design and pandemic response. Finally, he traces the development of museum and heritage attraction design through the key figures of John Ruskin, James Gardner and Alex McCuaig. Each chapter incorporates a key case study, with an international scope including examples from Hong Kong, the UK, Taiwan, Qatar, Dubai and Kuwait.

An essential introduction for undergraduate and graduate students taking courses in museum studies, heritage studies and tourism management.

Chris White is the Founder and Managing Director of Winkle-picker Ltd. He has provided interpretive and master planning services worldwide, particularly in London, Hong Kong and Singapore. He has been involved in the design of some of the world's most innovative multi-award-winning museums and exhibition projects.

"This important book is one of the first to integrate museum heritage and tourism. It examines the issue from a deep conceptual foundation and then translates this knowledge into a range of practical applications that are suitable for practitioners, students and the academic community. Written by a true global expert with many years of international experience, *Museum and Heritage Tourism: Theory, Practice & People* is a must-have resource."

Professor Bob McKercher, University of Queensland

"This unique and erudite book provides valuable insight into the crossover between museums, heritage and tourism. It is a welcome addition to the growing literature in heritage tourism studies and brings to light many of the challenges and opportunities associated with museum management and design, heritage management, and tourism. This work is a valuable asset to students and scholars throughout the world."

Professor Dallen Timothy, Arizona State University

Museums and Heritage Tourism

Theory, Practice and People

Chris White

LONDON AND NEW YORK

Designed cover image: [Getty]

First published 2023
by Routledge
4 Park Square, Milton Park, Abingdon, Oxon OX14 4RN

and by Routledge
605 Third Avenue, New York, NY 10158

Routledge is an imprint of the Taylor & Francis Group, an informa business

British Library Cataloguing-in-Publication Data
A catalogue record for this book is available from the British Library

ISBN: 978-1-032-43891-7 (hbk)
ISBN: 978-1-032-43890-0 (pbk)
ISBN: 978-1-003-36924-0 (ebk)

DOI: 10.4324/9781003369240

Typeset in Sabon
by Taylor & Francis Books

For Shelagh, Alfie and Ollie

Contents

Illustrations

Figures

Table

Boxes

Acknowledgements

I would like to thank all those people and organisations who have helped in providing case studies for the various chapters, in particular Chris Cawte of Design PM, Helen White of the Old Royal Naval College and Alex McCuaig of MET Studio. I would also like to thank Alex for his time, assistance and review of Chapter 9. Any errors are mine and mine alone.

Introduction

Before the COVID-19 pandemic crisis of 2020, travel, tourism and its associated activities accounted for one in four of all new jobs created across the world, 10.6 per cent of all jobs (334 million) and 10.4 per cent of global GDP (US$9.2 trillion), according to the World Travel and Tourism Council (WTTC). Even with the significant impact of the pandemic on the sector, it still accounted for 5.5 per cent of global GDP in 2020. A year later that share had crept up to 6.1 per cent and is continuing to grow. Taking into account the growth and diversification in recent decades, this makes tourism one of the most important sectors of the world economy.

It has been said that all travel is some form of cultural tourism. According to the definition adopted by the United Nations World Tourism Organisation (UNWTO) General Assembly of 2017, cultural tourism (and in this we can include heritage tourism) implies

> a type of tourism activity in which the visitor's essential motivation is to learn, discover, experience and consume the tangible and intangible cultural attractions/products in a tourism destination. These attractions/products relate to a set of distinctive material, intellectual, spiritual and emotional features of a society that encompasses arts and architecture, historical and cultural heritage, culinary heritage, literature, music, creative industries and the living cultures with their lifestyles, value systems, beliefs and traditions.

Cultural or heritage tourism, therefore, is both an established and growing driver of the world economy in both the "developed" and "developing" worlds.

However, the idea that the presence of museums or museum-like attractions contribute to the phenomenon of tourism, the role they play and how they do it remain subject to limited scholarly attention. In general, studies of museums in heritage and tourism are relegated to the

DOI: 10.4324/9781003369240-1

wider body of literature related to cultural and historical geography, anthropology, cultural studies and museology.

More personally, I have been working in the field of museum design and development for over 30 years. During this time, museums and heritage attractions have evolved to become cornerstones of national, regional and local tourism strategies. The significance of this can range from simply being a stop on a travel itinerary (and so contributing to a programme of activities to make a destination attractive to tourists) to being the sole catalyst of the revitalisation of the touristic appeal of an entire city or country (think the Guggenheim Bilbao or the National Museum of Qatar). So, undoubtedly a symbiotic relationship exists between museums, heritage attractions and tourism. Consequently, in recent years, I have been approached by various universities to advise on new hybrid courses that bring together elements of museum design, tourism and heritage management. However, when I went to the bookshelves to research possible topics and themes for the academic modules I found that no volume existed that looked at both the theoretical and the practical aspect of developing museums and heritage attractions within the context of the tourism market. There were either books on museology, books on tourism theory or books on museum design, but none that tried to take an overview of the interrelationship and interconnection between all these themes. This book aims to address this academic gap, to reach a wide audience of students, researchers and practitioners interested in heritage, tourism and museums, and to provide students and scholars with an accessible overview of some of the multidisciplinary issues in this field. Increasingly, due to the popularity of museum-like experiences as information providers or anchor attractions, people who may not come from a museum or tourism background are being asked to get involved in the commissioning and running of such projects, be that in the private or the public sector. This book is also intended for them.

Overall, the book is divided into three sections looking at the theories around history and heritage (and their application in museums for tourism), the practice of developing museums for tourism and some key figures in the field of heritage and museum design in the last 200 years. Each chapter contains a case study to provide a real-world example of the relevant issues under discussion.

The Theories section begins with Chapter 1 in which I look at the distinction between history and heritage, and discover that within each field there are profound disagreements amongst academics and practitioners about their definition, let alone how to compare them. My main focus, however, is to answer the question "What is heritage?". After tracing the evolution of the usage of the term, I discuss how heritage has been used (and misused), particularly with reference to museums, and ultimately how the idea of heritage has been internationalised. The importance of the application of heritage through tourism is examined in Chapter 2 through following the history of heritage tourism from the earliest times to the 21st century, as well as exploring how the heritage tourist consumes the product of heritage tourism. Taking this a step further, Chapter 3 looks specifically at the role and types of museums for tourism, how they have developed as attractions and the way they have contributed to urban revitalisation.

How heritage projects are practically developed for tourism is examined in the Practice section, beginning with Chapter 4 on interpretation. Otherwise known as interpretive planning, we look at the role that an interpretive planner plays in a museum or heritage design project, the importance of understanding your audiences, what interpretation is and does and how it sometimes gets "lost" in large, particularly commercially-driven, projects. The actual process of how museums and heritage attractions are put together has evolved since I began working in the industry over 30 years ago. Initially under the forensic but generous mentorship of MET Studio's Director of Research Deirdre Janson-Smith (formerly of the Natural History Museum, London), the company of which I myself was eventually to become a director was a leader in the field, bringing greater systematic rigour and professionalism to the design process. This evolution is explored in Chapter 5 with the addition of a case study on Kuwait's Abdullah Al Salem Culture Centre by Design PM, a leader in the field of specialist museum project management founded by a former Managing Director of MET Studio and colleague Chris Cawte. Finally in Chapter 6, at the end of this section, we look at the challenge that COVID-19 has posed to the world in general, as well tourism and museum visitation, measures to deal with it and potential future trends, with specific reference to the experiences of the Old Royal Naval College, Greenwich.

The world of museum and heritage attraction design is full of personalities. The People section features three key figures: from the 19th century John Ruskin, to the mid-20th century James Gardner to the modern-day Alex McCuaig. All have in some way profoundly influenced and continue to influence the way we see, interact with and experience the touristic and educational experience of this most pervasive and fascinating aspect of global tourism.

Part I

Theory

Introduction

To be involved in the development of museums for tourism and other associated activities such as project or event management, it is important to have a firm understanding of how museums have evolved in terms of their purpose, role and process. Why are they such driving forces in the tourist economy? What is their relationship with local and national heritage? Who do they speak for and to? Engaging with the history of museums within tourism is essential to grasp how they have been used and continue to be used to shape narratives and identities of peoples and subjects. Only with this perspective on the past can we critically appraise the way museums are being developed for tourism today, and how that might change in the future.

In doing this, we are not so much looking at the theory of museum development from a strictly museological point of view (there are many practical books for museum practitioners) but rather trying to provide an overview of issues that need to be considered by anyone whose career (academic or professional) may coincide with a museum-for-tourism project. Given the proliferation of museum-like projects (from the small corporate to the international Expo), this is an ever more likely scenario for a growing number of people who may never have considered a career in the museum field.

This Theory section is divided into three parts intended to build towards an understanding of how museums act as tourism products: "History vs heritage", "Heritage tourism" and "Museums as tourism attractions". The "History vs heritage" chapter tries to answer the essential question for all cultural attractions "What is heritage?" and looks at how many of the issues around this culminated in the case of the statue of Edward Colston in Bristol, England. In Chapter 2, we look at how this notion of heritage has been applied through the heritage

DOI: 10.4324/9781003369240-2

tourism economic sector with a case study of one of the best developed of these – the UK heritage tourism market. Finally in this section, we look at how museums have been developed as tourist attractions, particularly as contributors to urban revitalisation, with a case study of the National Museum of Qatar.

1 History vs heritage

What is history?

Answering this question can lead historians to come to blows, verbally at least. Between January and March 1961, the historian Edward Carr gave the George Macauley Trevelyan series of lectures at the University of Cambridge. As a result of this, *What is history?* (Carr, 1961) soon became a seminal text for those beginning the study of history. Certainly, when I was contemplating studying history at university, my sister, who was then studying history at Oxford, recommended it as essential reading in the mid-1980s. Carr draws a distinction between "historical facts" and "facts of the past" and rejects the role of accidents in history. He argues that historians themselves are the products of their time and so are compromised as honest brokers in determining what facts of the past become facts of history. For Carr, there was a clear sociological imperative for history, and it was only of interest if it could point the way to making good policy in the future, rather than for its own sake.

Many historians took this badly, as an attack on their impartiality and professionalism. Geoffrey Elton (1967) saw Carr's work as being characterised by dangerous relativism and pushed against the rising tide of social, cultural and post-colonial historical study. He was primarily concerned with the role of historians as reconstructors of events based on a rigorous analysis of documentary evidence. Hugh Trevor-Roper criticised Carr for his apparent historical determinism in not giving sufficient examination to alternative parts of events. While renowned historian of the Third Reich Richard Evans (2001) acknowledges the debt we owe Carr for highlighting the subjective nature of all historians, invigorating history in the 1960s and insisting upon the interconnectedness of history, he points out how limiting his view was that history must always have a politically relevant dimension.

In its simplest form, history is relatively easy to define. It is the study of the past. Historians do not invent people, places or events, this is the job of a

DOI: 10.4324/9781003369240-3

novelist. Historians rely on evidence, but every historical account has short-comings. It cannot possibly be comprehensive but rather seeks to present and explain aspects of "facts" and evidence. In doing this, it attempts to give meaning to events through the historian's own interpretation of them.

Of course, the search for historical accuracy can sometimes be confused with a search for "the truth". This single-version approach to history is what many of us were taught in the school classroom and has resulted in trenchant and inflexible positions being taken in discussions about our own history, in Britain's case particularly around issues of colonialism. This can be seen, for example, in the broadly generational division of opinion about the removal of statues to slave owners in Britain such as Bristol's Edward Colston (see Case study 1). In recent decades, there has been a concerted effort to present multiple layers and perspectives on history which has cer-tainly impacted on the kinds of stories and interpretation one finds in Western European and American museums. This does not mean that all historical perspective is given equal weight. Holocaust deniers, for instance, should not be given equal credence to those examining the causes, processes and outcomes of that catastrophic event due to the overwhelming historical evidence against their position.

The imperfection of historical accounts, however, pales in comparison to the deliberate manipulation or even invention of a kind of bogus his-tory to forge national identities. It is when history becomes "useful" that many of its most egregious mistakes are made. The misuse of history in nation building was identified as early as 1882 by French historian Ernest Renan (1823–92) in a lecture entitled "What is a nation?" when he said that "Forgetfulness, and I would even say historical error, are essential in the creation of a nation". An admirer of Renan, Eric Hobshawn proposed that myth and invention are essential to the politics of identity (Hobsbawn & Ranger, 1983). For example, nothing appears more essential to a national past than the pageantry surrounding British monarchy in its public ceremonies and displays. However, many of these seemingly ancient traditions only appeared in the late 19th and 20th centuries. These "inven-ted traditions" even come to embody the spirit of whole nations and often this history in action is regarded as our most treasured cultural expres-sions, which are beyond questioning or reproach. Indeed, they are seen as immutable heritage.

What is heritage?

If, as L.P. Hartley (1953) famously observed in the opening line of his best-known novel, "The past is a foreign country: they do things differ-ently there", then heritage is a postcard of that other place, a present-day snapshot in substance, thought and deed. All history is to a greater or lesser degree selective, and heritage is a subset of history. However, heritage is harder to pin down. Despite dealing with the often distant past, as a notion it has relatively recent origins. It boils down to those parts of history which people feel that they have inherited from the past and which they have some responsibility to pass down to their descendants in the future. Notions of heritage range from physical resources to a state of mind. A starting point for much of the literature on heritage defines it as what we inherit (and choose to preserve) from the past and use in the present; it does not simply exist but is actively saved, used and possibly abused. Although those portions of history which people feel are inherited can be abstract, such as Shakespeare or Liberty, modern usage tends to mean something rather more tangible like buildings, objects or landscapes. If only because these sorts of things take up physical space, a process of selection comes into play which carries with it a decision-making value system. Perhaps to a greater degree than history, therefore, heritage demands a process of conscious selection as to what to preserve. And, because it often involves public money and property, it is often highly politically charged. Timothy and Boyd (2003) offer a definition of the focus of heritage activity as being related to tangible, immovable resources (e.g. buildings or landscapes), tangible movable resources (e.g. museum artefacts) or intangibles (e.g. customs and festivals). According to Howard (2003), heritage can also be a discipline, commodity, source of identity or process that acts across many levels (from world to family), objects (nature, sites, activities, etc.) or people who perform or implement it (from owners to academics).

A sense of heritage is a modern phenomenon reflecting the post-Enlightenment experience of emerging national identities in Europe in the 18th and 19th centuries, and attempts to rationalise the past with new forms of national consciousness (Graham, Ashworth & Tunbridge, 2005). Right from these early beginnings, national governments recognised heritage as a powerful force and have invested in defining and shaping ideas of heritage in their interests. From its inception, heritage has had a political dimension imposed upon it.

However, some of the more interesting and resilient forms of heritage consciousness emerged from 19th-century European romantic notions of the primal and essential power of nature and landscape in shaping national character. In Britain, this led directly to a heritage conservation movement to preserve areas of outstanding natural beauty, born in the fells and lakes of Cumbria. Wordsworth began writing guide books to the Lake District in the north-west of England in the 1810s and summed up a desire for conservation of the area when he wrote that it was "a sort of national property, in which every man has a right and an interest who has an eye to perceive and a heart to enjoy" (Yoshikawa, 2016). A monument on the edge of Derwent Water commemorates the impact of another early promoter of conservation, John Ruskin (more of him in Chapter 7). Another denizen of the Lake District, Canon Hardwicke Rawnsley founded the Lake District Defence League in 1876 and worked with Octavia Hill to create the National Trust for Places of Historic Interest or Natural Beauty in 1895. The resulting National Trust Act of 1907 describes its aims as:

> To promote the permanent preservation, for the benefit of the nation, of lands and tenements (including buildings) of beauty or historical interest; and, as regards land, to preserve (so far practicable) their natural aspect.

There is a sense in these early definitions of heritage that it is more than a legacy or inheritance (which can after all be negative in the sense of historical "baggage"), but that it is positively beneficial, that it can be enjoyed and that there is shared ownership of it. This shared sense of heritage is seen as contributing to local, regional and national identities – essential to the 19th-century projects of European and American nation building. In these early heady days of the harnessing of heritage to do good, there was not yet the caution that "heritage benefits someone, and usually disadvantages someone else" (Howard, 2003). The rise of the professions of archaeology and architecture in the 19th century also gave a boost to the notion of what and how to conserve, providing an expert professional class willing to act as proponents and guardians of sites and monuments. A surge in conservation-related legislation across Europe in that century included the establishment of the Comité Historique in France in the 1830s and the passing of the Ancient Monuments Protection Act in England in 1882. However, we do not really find the use of the word "heritage" in his modern sense until the 1920–30s but it does not really come into common usage until the 1960s or 70s, and then as a very politically-charged concept.

In recent decades, the discourse around what and what is not "legitimate" heritage has been accused of having an elitist focus on the concerns and material culture of the upper and upper-middle classes, particularly in the Western European context. The efforts to conserve estates and stately homes are seen as embedding the idea of monumentalism, the demonstration of lineage and social achievement in the conservation movement from the outset.

The when of heritage stretches back to nineteenth-century values and cultural concerns, the where of this discourse may be found not only in Western Europe, but also more specifically in the authorial voices of the upper middle and ruling classes of European educated professionals and elites.

(Smith, 2008)

This "authorised heritage discourse" relies on a power relationship in society whereby keepers of expert knowledge (e.g. curators) combine with agencies of authority to pass judgement on what is and what is not deemed heritage. Wherever you are in the world, it is worth asking whether your own national or local heritage icons are the result of this sort of authorised heritage discourse.

The directing of heritage

The way you define heritage depends on the direction from which you approach it. The scion of a British aristocratic family may view the contents and customs associated with the ancestral "pile" very differently from the descendants of the gardener who worked in the grounds, the visitors who have paid at the door on a wet bank holiday, the curators who select and arrange the displays of artefacts that interpret the history of the site and the charitable organisations or government departments that might contribute to its upkeep. A complex web of meanings, intentions and perceptions stretching back decades if not centuries will inform each party's understanding of the importance (or otherwise) of preserving and explaining the history of the site. Whether the site represents the heritage of a meaningfully representative number of people of the society in which it is situated may itself be in dispute. Aristocratic heritage tends to be inflated or extended to be presented as the heritage of everybody.

Whilst we are not solely concerned with British stately homes, the fact that such a seemingly accepted symbol of heritage is open to such a wide range of questions and interpretations points to the range of issues that need to be explored when approaching any kind of accepted canon of heritage assets. That is not to say that country houses should not be preserved for architectural reasons, for instance, or for their fine works of art and unique garden landscapes, but we need perspective on and a lack of nostalgia about their history. The majority of people who visit these country houses and their forebears didn't live that sort of life and so it should be clear that what is *part* of the national heritage isn't *all* of the national heritage. What is regarded as national heritage turns out to be a much narrower thing in practice. It is often defined by the descendants of the ruling elite of an earlier era. The artefacts which have survived from a time when the ruling elite was more powerful in an aristocratic mode than it is now have been presented as being everybody's heritage objects. Notions of heritage are politically inflected and should be redefined generation after generation through different, more representative lenses.

This effect is of course magnified many times when considered globally or across cultures. Heritage and cultural tourism organisations may be seen as part of this heritage discourse of unequal power, even to some extent colluding to peddle "bogus history" on an unsuspecting public (Hewison, 1987). On arriving in the UK, for example, you are more

Figure 1.1 Hardwick Hall is one of the finest Elizabethan buildings in the country but does it, and other National Trust properties like it, represent everyone's heritage in England?
Source: Photograph by Jack Plant on Unsplash.

likely to be assailed by images encouraging you to visit sites associated with the fairytale aspects of monarchy rather than those associated with the suffragettes or trade unionism. Continuity is emphasised over struggle for progress. The visitation and management of the prescribed list of "must-see" heritage attractions reinforces their status, as well as widely accepted social and cultural meanings.

Given the lenses (national, religious, ethnic, class, gender, age, etc.) through which we view heritage (Howard, 2003), it is hardly surprising that the usefulness of manipulating heritage to meet a particular agenda is as old as civilisation itself. We have seen how the dominant heritage discourse is linked to the development of 19th-century nationalism and liberal modernity. Theories of Critical Discourse Analysis (CDA) reveal how language and unequal power relationships have constructed a legitimised version of heritage from the perspective of the dominant elites within society (Fairclough et al., 2004). Post-Enlightenment crystallisation of the notion of Britishness, for instance, as the highest expression of human progress led to a cultural narrative that enabled the rationalisation of expansionist policies – a kind of Darwinian cultural "survival of the fittest". In Europe, not only did a prescribed vision of a country's heritage become essential to a nation's identity but also new manifestations of heritage became symbols of collective achievement, conquest and struggle. As Rudyard Kipling, arguably the British Empire's poet laureate, opened Kim, his novel of colonial India:

> He sat, in defiance of municipal orders, astride the gun Zam-Zammah on her brick platform opposite the old Ajaib-Gher – the Wonder House, as the natives call the Lahore Museum. Who hold Zam-Zammah, that 'fire-breathing dragon,' hold the Punjab; for the great green-bronze piece is always first of the conqueror's loot.
>
> (Kipling, 1901)

Museums in municipal squares solemnified by monuments to the collective memories of the conquering elites spread across the capitals and provincial cities of global European empires. The idea of heritage, therefore, became associated as much with the charmingly bucolic as with the jackboot of colonialism. These sites of remembrance and museums expounding the dominant cultural narrative have become central to the "performance" of heritage. Museums in particular, with their scientific taxonomies and ethnographic categorisations, became vehicles for a narrative of progress and rationality.

Nor was it simply a matter of defining and preserving one's own nation's heritage. Other nations' heritage could be brought to one's shores and used to legitimise expansionist national identities and glorify adventure in foreign lands. The 1878 Monuments (Metropolis) Bill brought together some interesting strands of attitudes to heritage conservation and tourism in Victorian Britain. The Bill empowered "the Metropolitan Board of Works to accept and maintain the Obelisk known as Cleopatra's Needle and other Monuments, and to provide for the erection of the same on the Thames Embankment and on other lands". Presented to the UK by Muhammad Ali, ruler of Egypt and Sudan, in 1819 to commemorate Nelson's victory at the Battle of the Nile and Abercromby's victory at the Battle of Alexandria in 1801, the nearly 2,000-year-old obelisk remained in Alexandria until 1877 and was finally erected by the Thames on Victoria Embankment along with a time capsule of contemporary artefacts (including a set of photographs of the 12 best-looking English women of the day!). Another earlier example of British appropriation of another nation's material culture for (so the argument went) the sake of preservation was the removal of the sculptures and friezes from the Parthenon in Greece by Lord Elgin between 1801 and 1812. There was not universal agreement even amongst contemporary Britons about the validity of this supposed act of heritage conservation. No less a figure than Lord Byron (who was himself to die for the cause of Greek independence) wrote in *Childe Harold's Pilgrimage*

Dull is the eye that will not weep to see

Thy walls defaced, thy mouldering shrines removed

By British hands, which it had best behoved

To guard those relics ne'er to be restored.

Curst be the hour when from their isle they roved,

And once again thy hapless bosom gored,

And snatch'd thy shrinking gods to northern climes abhorred!

(Canto II stanza XV)

The Elgin (or Parthenon) Marbles first went on display in the British Museum in 1832 and are a subject of dispute between the British and Greek governments to this day. More widely, there is an increasing demand for the restitution of artefacts sacked from sites around the world by colonial powers that may well become the cultural issue of this century. Another case in point is the heated debate around the Benin

Figure 1.2 The Elgin Marbles at the British Museum have long been the focus of an ownership dispute between the British and Greek governments
Source: Photography by Xavier Von Erlach on Unsplash.

Bronzes – thousands of brass, bronze and ivory sculptures and carvings. Originally in southern Nigeria, they were (and let's not be mealy-mouthed about this) stolen by British soldiers in 1897. Most are now in Western museums and private collections. The British Museum, with roughly 950 Benin Bronzes, has come under particular criticism for its refusal to give them back, especially after London's Horniman Museum returned a number of Benin bronzes in November 2022. The Edo kings – the Obas – have campaigned for decades in vain for the Benin Bronzes to be returned. Heritage conservation and its uses for tourism, therefore, have geo-political dimensions that are long lasting and go far beyond the walls of the seemingly genteel world of the museum, touching on issues of colonialism, ownership, identity and legitimacy.

Box 1.1 Case study 1: The statue of Edward Colston

In the wake of the global condemnation of the murder of George Floyd by an American police officer and the Black Lives Matter (BLM) movement, slave trade-related statues were attacked in many cities around the world. The tearing down of Edward Colston's statue in

Bristol, England became worldwide news. A relatively unknown figure outside of the city (and even among many Bristolians), his unceremonious toppling into Bristol harbour by anti-racist activists caused ripples in a way that was far removed from the usual academic discussions in universities of empire and memorialisation. It struck deep at the heart of what is meant by "English history". Colston had made his name and his fortune as a 17th-century slave-trader, and later as an MP and philanthropist. Debates around the suitability of the statue were by no means new. The statue had been erected in 1895 but was the focus of controversy beginning in 1920 and intensifying towards the end of the 20th century. By 2014, nearly half of the people of Bristol wanted it removed and it became a regular target of graffiti and suggestions for amendment. On 7 June 2020, protestors pulled it down, daubed it with red paint and pushed it into the water. Nearly two years later, the perpetrators were acquitted of criminal damage by a jury. However, late that same year in September 2022, a court of appeal ruling stated that the acquitted could not rely on a human rights defence as the incident involved significant and violent criminal damage, and the case continues.

What were the wider consequences for the idea of heritage in Britain? What were the implications for the men (and they were predominantly men) who had been cast in bronze and mounted on plinths around the nation as testimony to their "great works"? Could things that seem such solid markers of our history, heritage and identity really be so open to change? What sort of sudden change to our heritage is acceptable and by whom? The statue itself raised questions that went right to the heart of the history vs heritage debate. It was erected nearly 200 years after Colston's death by merchants of the city for their own reasons and not necessarily those since attributed to it. It made claims for the "wise and virtuous son of the city" of Bristol but omitted entirely any reference to the 84,000 human beings he had traded as slaves, of which he was complicit in the death of 19,000. So, in one sense his statue represented poorly presented history and it would be hard to argue that Colston was a heritage worthy of respect by the Afro-Caribbean population of the city, or many others repulsed by Britain's involvement in the transatlantic slave trade.

These are deeply contentious issues for British society to deal with, but interestingly many people immediately turned to museums as the obvious place in which to reflect these debates. Indeed, Ray Barnett, Head of Collections at the Bristol Museums Service, went to the site of the now empty plinth on the day that it happened in order to collect BLM banners and placards to ensure they were preserved for the eventual contextualisation that he was sure would take place in a museum environment. The statue was raised from the River Avon and placed in the hands of the museum service which saw its role was to conserve the statue as an artefact like any other until a decision was taken as to what to do with it. In the summer of 2021, the

Figure 1.3 The Black Lives Matter (BLM) movement was sparked by the murder of George Floyd by on-duty Minneapolis police officer Derek Chauvin in May 2020
Source: Photograph by Rachael Henning on Unsplash.

statue of Edward Colston went back on public display at a Bristol
Museum called M Shed, this time as a very different sort of heritage
"to start a city-wide conversation about its future". It lies on its back
(the base has been damaged making it difficult to mount) surrounded
by the contextual ephemera of banners, placards and projected
headlines related to its toppling. The red paint with which it was
defaced has been left in place. The museum provides historical perspective about why the statue was erected in the first place, Colston's life and asks the public "What next?".

The resulting report by the Bristol History Commission showed
that four out five Bristol residents thought that the statue should be
displayed in a city museum and 70 per cent thought a plaque should
be added to the plinth reflecting the events of 7 June 2020 (Burch-
Brown & Cole et al., 2022). There can be few better examples of the
mutability of history and heritage and the ways in which museums
can be relevant in debates around these issues than the fate of
Edward Colston's statue.

The internationalisation of the idea of heritage

In 2005, the International Centre for the Study of the Preservation and
Restoration of Cultural Property (ICCROM) collected early definitions
and codification of cultural heritage. Pre-18th-century examples include a
letter written in the 6th century AD by Theoderic the Great to the Prefect
of Rome, the Papal Bull of Pius II in 1462 and the Antiquities Ordinance
passed by Charles XI of Sweden in 1666 (Jokilehto, 2005). Post-revolu-
tionary France then led the way with instructions and memos about
historic preservation in 1789–99, 1815, 1819 and 1830, until William
Morris's manifesto for the Society for the Protection of Ancient Buildings (SPAB) founded in 1877 defined a building as worth preserving if it
possessed "anything which can be looked on as artistic, picturesque,
historical, antique, or substantial: any work, in short, over which educated, artistic people would think it worth while to argue at all".

As European colonial rule spread across the world, so did European
concepts of heritage conservation and management to such an extent
that they became accepted orthodoxy. These ideas have been manifested
in various international agreements and charters. The leading world
body in this regard is the International Council on Monuments and Sites
(ICOMOS) which ascribes the growth in internationalism to the post-

World War I founding of the League of Nations (which included the International Commission on Intellectual Cooperation based in Geneva and later Paris, a fore-runner of the United Nations Educational, Scientific and Cultural Organisation (UNESCO)) and the post-World War II creation of the United Nations and UNESCO. ICOMOS sees the 1931 Athens Conference, which was organised by the International Museums Office and brought together conservationists of historic buildings, as fundamentally influential in establishing the concepts of conservation, such as the idea of a common world heritage, the importance of the setting of monuments and the principle of integration of new materials. Post-war reconstruction underlined that it was not simply a matter of listing and preserving historic buildings in isolation but that they had to be considered in their architectural environmental context. The First International Congress of Architects and Specialists of Historic Buildings held in Paris in 1957 made seven key recommendations including that countries should establish a central organisation for the protection of historic buildings, the creation of an international assembly of architects and specialists of historic buildings should be considered and that architects and town planners should cooperate to integrate historic buildings into town planning.

The second conference was held in Venice in 1964 and culminated in the Venice Charter which adopted 13 resolutions related to historic conservation. The five key principles it promoted were: the extension of the concept of historic buildings to both isolated buildings and groups of buildings; the conservation of buildings being "always facilitated by making use of them for socially useful purposes" (of particular relevance to the revitalisation of heritage tourism sites) but with no change to lay out or decoration; restoration to be done only when necessary using traditional techniques wherever possible; archaeology to only be carried out by specialists and the rehabilitation of such sites should not alter the buildings to enhance understanding; and all such actions should be documented and made public. The Convention Concerning the Protection of the World Cultural and Natural Heritage adopted in 1972 created a clear distinction between "cultural heritage" (defined as monuments, science and sites) and "natural heritage" (natural features, geological and physiographical features). Among other subsequent conventions and charters (for instance, for mural painting and cultural landscapes), the UNESCO Convention for Safeguarding of the Intangible Cultural Heritage defines intangible heritage as "the practices, representations, expressions, knowledge, skills – as well as the instruments, objects, artefacts and cultural spaces associated therewith – that communities, groups and, in some cases, individuals recognise as part of their cultural heritage". This shows significant progress from the 1931 conference but still did not deal with issues such as reversibility in restoration. The Venice Charter has been reviewed on a number of occasions in its 48-year history but still remains a touchstone for general principles in international heritage efforts.

Conclusion

Defining history can be a matter of discussion and even argument, but heritage is history that can be or has been activated. When activated, heritage can bring a sense of pride and identity to a location, as well as contribute to local, regional and national economies. However, we must be mindful of privileging an unrepresentative (often elite) group in society and presenting it as the heritage of the whole. The contentious nature of what heritage gets activated and for whom is ongoing as can be seen by the re-evaluation of colonial and slave-related statues and monuments in the UK and US following the activism of the BLM movement. Western notions of heritage, associated with 19th-century European nation building and how it should be treated, have been codified over the last 200 years and globalised, initially through imperialism and later through voluntary membership of transnational organisations. How heritage is activated by museums and heritage products and the issues around such activity are the subject of subsequent chapters.

References

Burch-Brown, J. & Cole, T. *et al.* (2022). *The Colston Statue: What next? We Are Bristol History Commission Short Report*. Bristol: Bridging Histories.

Carr, E.H. (1961). *What is history?* New York: Vintage.

Elton, G. (1967). *The practice of history*. London: Methuen.

Evans, R. (2001). The two faces of E.H. Carr. *History In Focus, Autumn Issue* 2.

Fairclough, N., Graham, P., Lemke, J. & Wodak, R. (2004). Introduction. *Critical Discourse Studies, 1(1)*.

Graham, B., Ashworth, G.J. & Tunbridge, J.E. (2005). The uses and abuses of heritage. In Corsane, G. (Ed.) *Heritage, museums and galleries: an introductory reader*. London: Routledge.

Hartley, L.P. (1953). *The go-between*. London: Hamish Hamilton.

Hewison, R. (1987). *The heritage industry; Britain in a climate of decline*. London: Methuen.

Hobshawn, E. & Ranger, T. (1983). *The invention of tradition*. Cambridge: Cambridge University Press.

Howard, P. (2003). *Heritage: management, interpretation, identity*. London: Continuum.

Jokilehto, J. (2005). *Definition of cultural heritage—references to documents in history*. Rome: ICCROM Working Group 'Heritage and Society'.
Kipling, R. (1901). *Kim*. London: Macmillan & Co.
Smith, L. (2008). *Uses of heritage*. Abingdon: Routledge.
Timothy, D.J. & Boyd, S.W. (2003). *Heritage tourism*. Harlow: Pearson Education.
Yoshikawa, S. (2016). *William Wordsworth and the invention of tourism, 1820–1900*. Abingdon: Routledge.

Further reading

Carr, E.H. (1961). *What is history?* New York: Vintage.
Smith, L. (2008). *Uses of heritage*. Abingdon: Routledge.

2 Heritage tourism

Tourism accounts for approximately 5 per cent of global GDP and is the world's largest service sector industry. As one of the fastest growing sectors in the world economy, it is one of the most important creators of new jobs – approximately one in twelve. It is the main export for a third of developing countries and in some small island states can represent 25 per cent of GDP. It is hard to estimate how much of this tourism is for the sole purpose of visiting a cultural or heritage site but estimates by the World Tourism Organisation (WTO) puts the desire to experience heritage places as a motivating factor for around 40 per cent of these trips. It also predicts an international tourism arrivals figure of around 1.8 billion in 2030.

Cultural or heritage tourism, therefore, is both an established and growing driver of the world economy in both the "developed" and "developing" worlds. It has been observed that all travel is some form of cultural tourism and that it is omnipresent (Richards, 2007). In broad terms, cultural tourism is travel for the purpose of learning or experiencing another culture (Adams & Roy, 2007), often in the sense that Williams (1958) envisaged culture – as a whole way of life. Since the end of the Second World War, the demand for cultural or heritage tourism experiences has increased dramatically, whether for reasons of religious pilgrimage, to visit places of literary, industrial or (increasingly) cinematic/televisual significance, to trace family heritage or to experience living cultures and festivals.

Tourism in the post-war modern era has continued to grow and expand its attainability. Indeed, the WTO characterises an average 6.5 per cent growth in tourist arrivals since 1950 as one of the most remarkable economic and social phenomena of the past century. And at an average of 13 per cent during this period (until COVID-19 struck such a heavy blow to the industry in 2020 and 2021), such phenomenal growth has been nowhere stronger than in Asia and the Pacific. Whilst the academic study of heritage tourism, along with other forms of

DOI: 10.4324/9781003369240-4

tourism, is a relatively recent phenomenon, the activity itself is clearly not. But what exactly is heritage tourism?

Defining heritage tourism

The territories of cultural and heritage tourism overlap very closely. Timothy (2011) gets around the issue of definition by resigning himself to the interchangeability of the terms and defining cultural heritage tourism as that which "encompasses built patrimony, living lifestyles, ancient artifacts and modern art and culture". Modern attempts to define heritage tourism tend to focus on its use of a heritage asset or assets, usually tangible but possibly supplemented by intangible elements, as the focus for the tourist experience. Smith (2009) characterises heritage tourism as being largely concerned with the interpretation and representation of the past and, as such, is a branch of cultural tourism that is a veritable political and ethical minefield.

From a management point of view there are three main classes of heritage assets: buildings and archaeological sites; heritage cities, routes and cultural landscapes; and movable cultural property and museums (McKercher & du Cros, 2002). The visitors themselves, however, do not tend to plan their visit according to these criteria. Looking at it from an attraction-driven visitor perspective, types of heritage tourism might break down into artistic, natural, living cultural, built, industrial, personal or dark heritage (Timothy & Boyd, 2003). Military and literary heritage attractions are also sometimes included as distinct genres. And there is considerable crossover between what might be seen as heritage and cultural tourism. Is a visit to a museum or viewing a performance in an ancient amphitheatre heritage or cultural tourism? Does it matter?

Given that, as we have seen in Chapter 1, heritage is the aspects of our surroundings, objects and traditions we have chosen to preserve, the idea of heritage tourism immediately raises the question of "What have we preserved for the purposes of this tourist visit and why?". Whereas cultural tourism is tourism with the purpose of experiencing another culture, heritage tourism (by virtue of the way it has developed) carries overtones of tourism for the purpose of endorsing preservation. To this end, studies over the past 20 years into the interaction between tourism and heritage assets have thrown up three main lines of enquiry: supply-side issues, demand-side issues and sustainability, impact and inclusion (Jansen-Verbeke & McKercher, 2010).

It is also important to consider exactly who is defining what we frame and construct as heritage worth preserving. As essentially a visual, tangible and material phenomenon, aesthetes and experts, connoisseurs and

Figure 2.1 This fibreglass teddy bear in front of the revitalised Marine Police
    Headquarters in Tsim Sha Tsui, Hong Kong may be what conserva-
    tionists mean when they talk about the "Disneyfication" of heritage
Source: Photograph by Chris White.

curators have come to dominate the debate on what is and what is not
"heritage", resulting in a reliance on their associated skills of interpretation,
presentation and representation in a tourism context (Waterton & Watson,
2010). This creates a self-perpetuating and self-referential set of definitions
that can risk becoming overbearing orthodoxy.

Heritage conservationists bristle at the notion that tourism has somehow rescued heritage which might otherwise have disappeared, fearing
presumably the "Disneyfication" or watering down of heritage for the
consumption of visitors. Howard (2003) typifies this view: "Heritage has
many markets, only one of which is the tourist. The tourist market may
have a deep pocket, but much heritage is not designed for them ...". In
his view, the idea that heritage = tourism needs to be resisted.

A woefully incomplete history of cultural/heritage tourism

> Human history is the story of a traveler, an Odysseus.
>
> (Williams, 1998)

The analysis of the skeleton of a prehistoric teenage boy from the north coast of the Mediterranean buried at Stonehenge in England is a reminder how far human beings have always travelled to see an iconic tourist attraction. Indeed, "ongoing scientific research suggests that around 30 per cent of the wealthiest individuals buried around the Neolithic and Bronze Age temple came from hundreds and, in some cases, thousands of miles away" (Keys, 2010).

If, as some have stated, cultural tourism is ubiquitous throughout human history, any attempt to give an overview of its development is a thankless task. Given that the modern study of tourism as an academic discipline in earnest can only really be traced back to the 1960s (Tribe, 1997) and that the vast majority of evidence is available only from the written record of letters, journals, books and novels (hence narrowing the contributors to a select band of the educated literati), we are restricted to looking at a relatively limited body of work on the evolution of the types of cultural heritage assets, the way they have been experienced or consumed and by whom. The almost ridiculous hubris required to embark on a review of such a sweeping phenomenon is like trying to represent the history of global cuisine using a single basket of dim sum. The sample of flavours presented below is harvested from available relevant literature, mental clippings from 40 years of formal education and interest in travel and serendipitous discoveries in libraries, newspapers and conversation.

Cultural tourism in Ancient Egypt, Greece and the Roman Empire

It is reasonable to assume that as soon as we had money and wheels, as the Sumerians (or Babylonians) did around the beginning of 4000 BCE, cultural tourism began. Casson (1994) points to evidence of tourism in Egypt as early as 1500 BCE, whilst Adams and Roy (2007) dispute whether anything we could genuinely call cultural tourism existed in earlier periods in Egypt due to the Egyptians' sense of cultural superiority. In terms of written evidence of cultural tourism, Elsner and Rutherford (2005) state that as early as the 3rd Millennium BCE Gudea of Lagash from Sumer (Southern Mesopotamia or modern-day Iraq) records a journey to visit the sanctuary of the goddess Nanshe some distance away. There is certainly evidence of the phenomenon of cultural tourism beginning in earnest in the Graeco-Roman period (Adams & Roy, 2007).

The Greek conquest of much of the known world by the 4th century BC gave tourists of Ancient Greece access to the civilisations of the Egyptians, Persians and Babylonians. It also spurred the development of repositories of valuable objects, or museums. The "Top Ten" style of tourist guide can be traced to this time with various writers including Herodotus (c. 484–425 BCE), Philo of Byzantium (c. 280–220 BCE), Diodorus of Sicily (60?–30? BCE), Strabo (64/63 BCE–c.24 CE) and perhaps most prominently Antipater of Sidon (?2nd century BCE) contributing to a list of must-see attractions commonly known as the Seven Wonders of the Ancient World. Manmade temples, monuments and colossi (one can easily imagine the Hanging Gardens of Babylon or the Lighthouse of Alexandria being a tourist draw in our age) were promoted far and wide; indeed just as the sole surviving wonder, the Great Pyramid of Giza, is today.

Why should all of the concerns around contemporary heritage tourism – motivations, definitions, protection, management, authenticity, interpretation, access value – not have been just as much of an issue in the ancient world? Casson (1994) believes they were and provides us with examples of each. Despite these earlier sightseeing writings, the first Western culture to verifiably engage in mass tourism as we would recognise it was Imperial Rome (27 BCE–476 CE) (Feiffer, 1985). A borderless tourist zone was made possible by the Pax Romanus stretching from Hadrian's Wall in the far north of England to the Euphrates. Tourists (usually combining their travel with some form of official duty), who may have had their interest piqued by displays of obelisks (echoes of which we see later in 19th-century imperial London) or war booty from Asia on the streets of Rome, could stay at inns along roads frequently as good as they were in the 18th century. Travel for leisure soon became widespread enough for the Stoic philosopher Seneca (4 BCE–64 CE) to write cynically in *De Tranquillitate Animi* about young men indulging in such pursuits as a diversion from everyday life: "One journey after another they embark on, one spectacle they exchange for another. As Lucretius says, 'Thus each man flees himself'" (Davie, 2007). The desire to experience the remotely exotic in established cultural tourism destinations is an early motivation and the object of active promotion by the 1st century CE:

> there are a great many things in Rome and nearby which we have never seen nor even heard of, though if they were to be found in Greece, Egypt or Asia, or any country which advertises its wealth of marvels, we should have heard and read about them and seen them for ourselves.
>
> (Pliny the Younger (61–112CE) in Letter 8.20, Gerolemeu, 2018)

Adams and Roy (2007) use the tour of Germanicus Caesar (13 BCE–19 CE), as reported by Tacitus (Annals 2.59–61), to exemplify a typical

Figure 2.2 Can anyone doubt that the Great Pyramid of Giza or the Statue of the Sphinx have been the focus of some form of heritage tourism for around 4,500 years?
Source: Photograph by Sumit Mangela on Unsplash.

tourist itinerary to Egypt in 19 CE and highlight the principal types of tourist attractions – the party town of Canopus, the "talking" statue of Memnon, the pyramids (with the inevitable guides and trinket sellers), the Nile's artificial lake, the irrigation channels of the Fayum, sacred crocodiles, gorges and former frontier cities. Here, tourism is not a reverent pursuit but one of amusement, entertainment and wonder. Other tourist attractions at this time according to Greek historians Strabo and Diodorus include the Labyrinth, thought to be the temple of Amenemhet III at Hawara, the city of Thebes and the memorial temple of Pharoah Ramesses II.

The colonial nature of much of both Greek and Roman tourism is echoed in later Victorian British cultural tourism – an inquisitiveness about the conquered cultures of Egypt and Greece, a desire to fit their cultural glories within a Roman narrative of superiority and not a little condescension.

European medieval pilgrimage

Pilgrimage (both religious and secular) is sometimes hard to distinguish from cultural tourism and possibly it is unnecessary. There is evidence of pilgrimage motivated by religious curiosity or worship to temples and shrines in the Ancient World, but it is the European Middle Ages (c. 5th–15th centuries) that conjure up the most evocative, Chaucerian images of organised travel for religious purposes. Itinerant devotion began in earnest in the 7th century and reached its apogee in the 12th–14th centuries (Swatos & Tomasi, 2002).

Certainly, pilgrimage was religious in nature but has more than a hint of prototypical medical tourism; healthy pilgrims simply with an interest in seeing the sights and getting some absolution from sin in the bargain were joined on the road by the hobbling and stretchered infirm moving between a network of hostels, monasteries, shrines and hospices. The proliferation of relics at religious locations along the way and the burgeoning souvenir trade are testimony to the economic benefits that were a side-effect of such cultural tourism. A "must-see" reliquary was a prerequisite to making profit from tourism, much like a collection of priceless artefacts in a modern museum. We would now refer to it in tourism terms as an attraction.

From Western Europe, some journeys were immensely long and only for the rich, to the Holy Land for instance. Some were relatively short, such as the journey from the Tabard Inn in Southwark to the shrine of Thomas Beckett in Canterbury described by Geoffrey Chaucer (c.1343–1400) at the end of the 14th century in the *Canterbury Tales*. Having undertaken his own cultural tourist trip in 1373 to Florence to hear inspirational lectures given by Boccaccio about the *Decameron*, Chaucer wrote this fictionalisation of the usually earthly (and earthy) concerns of pilgrims which provides us with a lively, contemporary insight into the mixed motivations of a middle-class tour group to one of the foremost heritage attractions in England. This ribald account undermines any pretence that medieval pilgrimage was all about penance, purification and purging, and that the post-16th-century Reformation "modern" traveller re-invented the journey as pleasure and personal experience (Leed, 1991). Religion might have been the motivation for many pilgrims, but that didn't mean they couldn't have a good time. The pilgrimage became a vehicle for creating narratives – drinking, flirting and more – along the way, the medieval equivalent of a prolonged stag do or hen party with Chaucer breaking the golden rule that "what goes on tour stays on tour". But the Reformation, Renaissance and Enlightenment in Europe undoubtedly led to both a greater desire for personal fulfilment and an aspiration to broaden the mind by experiencing the fruits of a revolutionary flowering of cultural creativity and production – perhaps best represented by the Grand Tour.

The European Grand Tour

The idea of tourism as self-enriching rather than soul-preserving comes truly into vogue between the 16th and 18th centuries (and of course continues today). The Grand Tour, a term first used in the French translation of a *Voyage or a Compleat Journey* through Italy by Richard Lassels published in 1670, encompassed experience (including sexual), education and exchange of ideas, creating the largest and most independent wandering "academy" – a sort of mobile finishing school – that Western civilisation has ever known (De Seta, 1996).

Pursuing Francis Bacon's (1561–1626) idea expressed in 'Of Travel' that "travel, in the younger sort, is a part of education, in the elder, a part of experience" (Williams, 1992), young aristocrats, members of the upper-middle class and bursaried students travelled to gain knowledge – of the arts, literature, ancient and modern history, commerce, diplomacy, music, the theatre, local customs and sexual mores. The character of the tour changed over time from the earlier classical Grand Tour with its focus on a prescribed list of galleries, museums and artefacts to a more private engagement encompassing the scenic sublime in the 19th-century romantic version (Towner, 1985), including the development of a network of spa towns.

A largely elitist pursuit in the 18th century, by the late 19th century the removal of the young educated classes to the Continent to complete their education represented something of an exodus – the prototype "gap year". These "lay pilgrims who followed ancient routes of knowledge" (Swatos & Tomasi, 2002) provided demand that built a tourist infra- structure we can still recognise today. The experience of the journey inclu- ded the people you met along the way such as the dons, tutors, cousins and old servants described in John Ruskin's *Praeterita*, arguably as important as the cultural sites themselves (Adams & Roy, 2007). Initially primarily focused on Italy, the itinerary expanded to include France, the Swiss Alps and Savoy – so spawning the traditional reputation for excellence of the modern European hotel industry. By the late 18th century in the relatively remote Alpine region of the Tyrol, "the hospitality industry surpassed all other trades in topographical presence and density" (Heiss, 2002). New infrastructure and amenities would be necessary due to the re-discovery and making accessible of sites of classical interest such as Herculaneum (1738) and Pompeii (1748), drawing tourists ever further afield. Accommodation, from small hotels such as the Pensione Bertolini described in E.M. Forster's *A Room with a View* to the grand hotels in Europe that began to appear in the mid-19th century, would have relied on the sustainability of its cultural destination and attractions as much as any tourist hotel today.

In the Victorian era, cultural tourism in Britain and Europe had pro- found economic consequences. As railway networks exploded across Europe in the 19th century, hotels, frequently luxurious or "grand", became an established part of large railway companies' businesses (Wolmar, 2009). By the middle of the 19th century, the age of the European grand hotel was truly underway, bequeathing us names such as the Hotel du Louvre (opened in Paris, 1855), the Savoy (London, 1889) and the Ritz (Paris, 1898 and London, 1906). This influence of European hospitality was formalised into a replicable form through the creation of what is regarded as the first spe- cialist hospitality school of its kind in Europe at Lausanne in 1893, which was followed in other countries such as Portugal, France and the United Kingdom (UK). From Edinburgh to Istanbul, hotels opened in this golden age still represent iconic benchmarks of luxury in the hospitality industry.

Chinese forms (Tang – Qing dynasties)

> The man of wisdom takes pleasure in water; the man of humanity delights in the mountains.
>
> (Confucius, *The Analects*, VI.21, Knowles, 2001)

From the Tang (618–907) to the Qing (1644–1912) dynasties, Chinese tourism has a tradition independent of Europe. Travel by educated people (predominantly men on official business) between the outposts of an expanding empire and the capital is known in China as early as the Zhou period (1046–256 BCE) (Zhang, 2011). At the heart of traditional travel culture in China, was landscape appreciation by an increasingly Taoist-influenced elite literati, rather than the European inquisitiveness for social encounters (Yan, 2010). In this regard, the natural attractions of mountains were the main draw, acting as objects of contemplation and self-cultivation. When time was against them, these scholars used the suburban outskirts of cities as substitutes for remote wanderings, developing an appreciation for a range of landscapes closer to home (Gerritsen, 2007). During this period straightforward landscape prose was developed that would later influence the development of travel diaries (*Youji*), but Hargett (1989) puts Li Ao's *Register of Coming South* (*Lainan lu*) forward as a candidate for the first recognisable prose narrative of a journey (undertaken in 809 CE) in diary form in China.

The expansion of the government civil service examination system, requiring as it did the need for travel both to study for and take the exams, as well as the taking up of government posts in the Tang (618–907) and particularly the Song (960–1279) dynasties, increased opportunities for sightseeing. Zhang (2011) states that it is clear from innumerable accounts by Song literati travellers that visiting famous mountains and beautiful rivers (*mingshan shengjing*) and famous historical sites (*shengji*) was regarded as an activity quite separate from official missions and seen as an essential way to broaden the mind and cultivate the moral self. Hargett (1989) sees the Song as the most important period in the development of *youji*, including daytrip essays, embassy accounts and river diaries. Fan Chengda (1126–1193), for instance, a particularly prolific travelling official and poet, wrote a detailed account (*Wu-ch'uan lu*) of the scenic and historic sites he encountered on a boat journey he made in 1177 from Chengdu to Pingjiang (modern Suzhou), which took 122 days to complete covering 1,700 miles. And, just as rarity today confers status on and motivation to see a heritage object, so Fan notes when describing some fine sutras at the White River Monastery that "today one no longer sees this type of embroidery pattern" (translation in Mair, 1994).

Not that scholars were the only travellers on the road. Merchants were also a distinct travelling class in late imperial China, although their travel guides suggest they were more concerned about crime than sightseeing (Lufrano, 1997). But (as with so much history of the unlettered which disappears) the voices of the literati are those that have survived and come down to us in the written word. As innumerable poems suggest, tourist experiences were seen as transformative, almost becoming intangible artefacts of the scholar's studio to be turned over in the mind and reminisced about on a moonlit night under the influence of warm rice wine.

Nor were these scholar-travellers simply passive observers but, as testified by Fan Chengda, they actually enhanced the heritage status of the sites they visited by memorialising them in poetry, which they might even engrave on a column of a shrine or on a rock in the mountainside, returning years later to see if it had stood the test of time. These refined graffiti artists display a sense of the mutability and malleability of heritage quite unlike their Western counterparts. But that is not to say that conservation was not foremost in their minds when visiting these heritage sites. Zhang (2011) recounts examples of Song scholar-travellers actively lobbying local officials for fences to be erected to protect famous inscriptions, and the contribution of tourism to the Song economy was acknowledged.

During the Qing 1770s, there was an attempt to register all the temples in China and route books for tourists were increasingly available. By then, touristic pilgrimage to famous mountain sites was undertaken by emperors and common people, Han Chinese and ethnic minorities alike, so becoming a unifying factor in Chinese society (Naquin & Rawski,

Figure 2.3 An aerial view of the Ming dynasty (1368–1644) Humble Administrator's Garden. The Scholars' Gardens of Suzhou, China have been the subject of a form of tourism for around 1,000 years
Source: Photograph by Jerry Bao on Unsplash.

1987). Local history projects also proliferated with Qing provincial officials dispatched to find and record sites of stone stelae (inscribed tablets), old monasteries and pagodas, famous events, graves of famous people and natural landscapes that had been immortalised in well-known paintings or poems. A visit to these stelae would not necessarily have just been a nostalgic act as the emperors Kangxi (1662–1723) and Qianlong (1735–1799) were busy erecting tablets bearing inscriptions that laid down the law for subjugated peoples to justify imperial conquest (Perdue, 2005). They would have been overtly political sites viewed with a sense of national pride (or humiliation depending on your viewpoint) by many tourists, much as many contested heritage tourism sites are today.

This Chinese form of elite tourism bestowed a kudos upon these sacred places, but also culturally changed and created them, physically and imaginatively. However, Winter, Teo and Chang (2009) point out that on a conceptual level the historical growth of tourism in Asia has not been theoretically mapped and framed to the same extent as Western phenomena of the Grand Tour or package tours.

The 20th and 21st centuries

> If you are lucky enough to have lived in Paris as a young man, then wherever you go for the rest of your life, it stays with you, for Paris is a moveable feast.
>
> (Hemingway, 1964)

By the outbreak of the First World War in 1914, a considerable infrastructure of resorts was in place served by a network of railways and other forms of transport, including transatlantic cruise traffic, attractions, organisations such as agents and marketing practices. The mechanised mass slaughter of over 10 million soldiers during World War I (1914–18) gave rise to an understandable desire to live life to the full when peace came amongst those with disposable income. Between the wars in Europe, the increased ownership of cars, the prevalence of buses and the advances in passenger aviation meant greater movement of tourists which can be seen as a "rehearsal" for the take-off of tourism after the Second World War (Lickorish and Jenkins, 1997). The heyday of the travel poster displays the sheer range of destinations advertised (from Clacton-on-Sea to Cairo) and modes of transport (from trains and ocean liners to zeppelins) available and is testament to the explosion of travel for a wide range of people. The growth of mass political movements such as fascism and communism encouraged (and perhaps coerced) domestic and foreign supporters to visit purpose-built resorts in

Figure 2.4 Les Deux Magots café in Paris frequented by Hemingway who described the memories made whilst living in the city as "a moveable feast"

Source: Photograph by Sebastiaan Stam on Unsplash.

large numbers (Zuelow, 2016). The inter-war years (though no one at the time thought of them that way of course) saw the darkest of dark tourism as relatives travelled across Europe and further afield (my own great uncle is buried in the Commonwealth War Cemetery in Gaza) to visit war graves.

By 1938, Imperial Airways had a route network of 25,000 miles, flying at a conservative estimate 50,000 people around the British Empire between 1930 and 1938 (although it is hard to say what proportion of these would have had tourism as their main aim or included some form of tourism in their itineraries). Some half a million used the other European operators (Pirie, 2004). This was an era of expanding domestic tourism as well as international tourism; the era of the charabanc taking workers granted paid annual leave by enlightened industrialists, such as

George Westinghouse, to the seaside or countryside and the heyday of the pleasure pier (a successful example of a mass cultural tourism attraction if ever there was one). British working classes took part in working holidays, for example, over a quarter of a million Londoners make an annual trip to Kent for "hopping" or hop picking (in which my own father participated with his family as a child).

As well as travelling for business, necessity and tourism, a certain bohemian class of artists and writers began travelling with the express purpose of immersing themselves in other cultures. Was Ernest Hemingway a cultural tourist in the Paris of the 1920s? He was certainly to all intents and purposes a resident, living and working in the city with his first wife Hadley; but the "moveable feast" epigraph of his memoirs of that time suggests a motivation that might be attributable to many a cultural tourist. Might the idea of a moveable feast – an experience so rich that you can draw intellectual and emotional sustenance from it many years later – be a common theme that links Gudea of Lagash, medieval pilgrims to the Holy Land, Chinese scholars, Grand Tourists and Victorian aesthetes with self-proclaimed travellers on the hippy trail in India, Saga holiday cruisers around the classical sites of the Mediterranean and the trance party-goers in Thailand in the early 21st century?

Jet engines, increased wealth in the industrialised world and innovations such as credit cards led to an unprecedented period of post-Second World War tourism growth that showed little sign of abating into the 21st century until the global COVID-19 pandemic of 2020–21. However, the pursuit of the heritage tourism dollar led many cities in the 1970–90s to create pastiche versions of a simplified past in "a cynical desire to attract tourists by giving them what they want, something that seems genuinely old but that is in fact standardized and cookie-cutter" (Zuelow, 2016). How we might avoid this is looked at in subsequent chapters. Today, it is not unreasonable to assume that most holiday packages aimed at the general tourist include some element of heritage attraction. Indeed, these are often the most popular motivating elements of tourism products, making cultural tourism a continuing cornerstone of one of the largest industries in the world.

The heritage tourist and consumption

We all know who they are but we don't want to be known as one. Weary communities in cultural tourism destinations tend to throw up stereotypes as a way of humorously dealing with the seasonal invasion of well-meaning but intrusive souvenir hunters and photo opportunity snappers; so that the contemptuous Brit outside the Tower of London who ridicules the blue rinse American culture vultures is by the same token referred to by the locals as a typical farang on a Pattaya beach.

Touted as the world's bestselling travel book and *New York Times* bestseller, the popularity of *1000 Places to See Before You Die* (Schultz, 2011) revealed a widespread bucket list, train-spotting mentality towards cultural tourism. So, the acquisitive nature of mass cultural tourism makes consumption an appropriate word to use here. The classic image of cultural tourism is still closely tied to the European model of middle-class, passive consumption of historic sites and museums (Richards, 2007). A place, a site, a dance, a food does not seem to have been truly experienced until it has been photographed, videoed, posed with, thoroughly gawked at and often replayed to an appreciative group of tourists, all with similar photographs, videos and experiences. Social media and the Instagram generation have only amplified this phenomenon. However, beneath the sometimes crass manifestation of the desire to possess iconic experiential imagery is a noble idea – to learn (however superficially) about another culture. There are worse things to be doing on holiday.

It should be remembered that tourism is primarily a commercial activity or, more accurately, a collection of activities, that involves the consumption of experiences or that provides entertainment (possibly in the form of learning opportunities). Cultural heritage attractions act as magnets to tourists, some with a more powerful pull than others, that work together with other destination offers, and require management. Interestingly, something that reveals cultural tourism assets as worthy of study from a commercial standpoint is that they are not all attractions; whilst they may be culturally significant assets locally, they may not be realised as a cultural heritage resource. The Turin Shroud, for instance, supposedly the burial cloth of the crucified Jesus of Nazareth rediscovered in the 14th century, did not become a global sensation until Secondo Pia's 1898 photograph of it revealed it in negative. Turin has been benefitting from the resulting pilgrim trade ever since. If a locale actively wants to develop, market and manage such a cultural asset, this can be studied and theoretically modelled, as can any phenomenon that is classified as part of the tourism industry.

So often couched as an exploitative relationship between first world tourists and innocent locals that corrupt and distort a supposedly pre-existing pristine state of authenticity, McKercher and du Cros (2002) posit that some basics of tourism theory need to be borne in mind before drawing sometimes subjective and emotion-driven conclusions. For one thing, certain cultural tourism activities attract both international and local tourists. Indeed, local tourists (who do not fall into the traditional definition of tourists as people away from home staying at least one night) are an important target audience for repeat visits to heritage attractions, as are school groups in the area.

Box 2.1 Case study 2: The UK heritage tourism market

As we have seen, defining what constitutes a heritage tourist is difficult but the market is huge. This is especially true in the UK. Tourism is worth £127bn a year to the UK economy, around 9 per cent of GDP, and is the UK's third largest service export. Before the COVID-19 crisis that began in 2020, the sector was projected to grow 3.8 per cent a year until 2025, faster than the digital industry. The sector accounts for roughly 10 per cent of all jobs in the country, delivering economic growth in every city and region in the UK. VisitBritain, responsible for promoting tourism in the UK, regards cultural tourism as the most important part of the country's tourism sector, touching as it does some aspect of every trip to the country. The majority of respondents from 20 countries year after year agree that history and culture strongly influenced their choice of holiday destination with culture and heritage accounting for billions of pounds of spending by inbound visitors annually, more than a quarter of all spending by international visitors.

With an estimated 5–6,000 visitor attractions in England alone this is hardly surprising. According to a report aimed at increasing tourists from Brazil, China and Italy (VisitBritain, 2016), 43 per cent of holidaymakers visit museums or galleries (as high as 61 per cent for tourists from Brazil). The size of the UK's heritage tourism sector is bigger than the advertising, film or car industries. And what are they spending their money on? VisitBritain previously focused on three key pillars – cultural heritage (e.g. Shakespeare), Built or Historical Heritage (e.g. the Tower of London) and Contemporary Culture (e.g. modern art, theatre), but increasingly segments the offer into cultural heritage (e.g. Shakespeare, museums, pubs, sports, royalty, diversity) and contemporary culture (e.g. modern art, theatre, music). Historical-related culture was by far the most appealing of the offers. Chinese tourists ranked the royal family as the key draw to the UK followed by Shakespeare, British food, Sherlock Holmes and the London Underground. For Italians and Brazilians, London's Underground held great enticement with both groups ranking it as the most appealing aspect of British culture. Brazilians continued on the transport theme ranking red double-decker buses as the second most interesting thing to do and see, followed by the Beatles, pubs and food. Italians were keen on finding out more about British myths and legends, followed by pubs, red double-decker buses and afternoon tea. Addressing these perceptions and expectations of the UK's cultural tourism products across global tourist markets is increasingly vital to project the nation's "soft power" in an effective and powerful way, ever more important in post-Brexit Britain.

McKercher and Cros (2002) suggest five types of cultural tourist – the purposeful tourist (culture is the prime motivator), the sightseer (interested in culture but satisfied with a shallower experience), the serendipitous tourist (stumbling across a deep cultural experience by chance), the casual tourist (weakly motivated and seeking a shallow experience) and the incidental tourist (for whom culture is not a stated motive but who visits nevertheless). As so often with a lifestyle and life-stage driven activity, whilst it is useful for the industry to try to analyse the heritage tourism market, sometimes it is better to just appreciate its diversity and dynamism (Smith, 2009).

Tourists, or in this case consumers, use destinations as prisms through which to satisfy socio-psychological needs (Crompton, 1979). These can range from a simple impulse to "get away from it all", a mind-broadening ambition to "see the world", the desire to boast at dinner parties, a longing for interaction with new social equals or the postmodern journey to find oneself. These motivations will affect where we choose to go and what we choose to do when we get there. A constant, however, seems to be the desire for the exotic and authentic (MacCannell, 1989), the eternal search for the sacred. Much like secular pilgrims or modern-day *homo viator* (Swatos & Tomasi, 2002), we can transform a mundane scene for a local person (such as a kiss in a Paris street) into an iconic image embodying an archetype (romance) through the medium of the tourist's gaze (Urry, 1990). It is the tourist industry's role to predict these inspirations and create products to satisfy them in a fast-changing, ever more connected world. Park and Choi's (2011) study of tourist attitudes to visiting Gyeongbok Palace in South Korea shows that four dimensions affected their satisfaction and post-visit intentions, namely historicity, education, convenience and experience. In particular, historicity influenced their intention to visit, whilst cultural assets, historical buildings and traditional ceremonies affected visitor satisfaction, intention to return and intention to recommend.

Obviously, in order to have a heritage tourism draw you need to have preserved some heritage in the first place. Hong Kong is an interesting example in this regard. Post-war Hong Kong has been notoriously unsentimental about its built heritage. It is one of the world's ultimate urban landscapes and has a mature tourism market with well-established as well as recently completed heritage attractions; this is despite a relative lack of heritage assets compared to other world cities. In the last 50 years, heritage conservation policy in Hong Kong has moved from a narrow focus on pre-Colonial archaeology to a broader, more inclusive approach that incorporates wider geographic areas (i.e. districts) rather than individual buildings. There has been a growing appreciation of the value of cultural and heritage assets (as witnessed by the increased public activism since the removal of the Central Star Ferry in 2006) resulting in more built heritage assets being considered by the government as heritage assets for adaptive re-use as new venues of entertainment, education and the arts. The importance of built heritage conservation to both the identity of the people and city of Hong Kong, as well as the tourist industry, has been recognised in the last decade or so. Indeed, the relationship between heritage and identity has become something of a political lightning conductor in Hong Kong. We can now see the maxim of "adapt or die" being applied in the revitalisation of heritage buildings for a variety of uses. However, this approach is a relatively recent phenomenon and it remains to be seen how successful the Hong Kong government will be in implementing it. There are already examples such as the Marine Police Headquarters in Tsim Sha Tsui completed in 2009 to reflect upon which experts in the field agree fell short of expectations in many ways; it is more often cited as an example of how not to adaptively re-use a heritage site that has served as a warning for subsequent projects. At the end of 2017, the Blue House cluster in Wanchai, providing residential and community services, won the Award of Excellence in the UNESCO Asia-Pacific Awards for Cultural Heritage Conservation. The revitalisation of Tai Kwun, the former police headquarters, magistrates' court and prison, into a heritage and arts hub opened in 2016 is also seen as a much more successful example. In 2019, it received the Award of Excellence in the 2019 UNESCO Asia-Pacific Awards for Cultural Heritage Conservation for its conservation and revitalisation efforts. Starting from a position of low value ascribed to heritage assets, these projects show that developments in Hong Kong are at least starting to go in the right direction.

Conclusion

Tourism in some form or other is as old as human civilisation. It is a global phenomenon with provable roots as far back as the mid-second millennium BCE. The study of tourism itself, beginning in the late 20th century, has given us an insight into what an intrinsically human activity it is, how heritage tourism products have developed and evolved, and what a key industry it is in the world economy. Cultural or heritage tourism is now a major economic force worldwide with an increasing and ever evolving understanding of its motivations, purposes and ways to fulfilment. How museums fit into this picture will be looked at in the next chapter.

References

Adams, C. & Roy, J. (Eds.). (2007). *Travel, geography and culture in Ancient Greece, Egypt and the Near East.* Oxford: Oxbow.

Casson, L. (1994). *Travel in the Ancient World.* Baltimore, MD: Johns Hopkins University Press.

Crompton, J. (1979). Motivations for pleasure vacation. *Annals of Tourism Research*, 6(4), 408–424.

Davie, J. (2007). *Seneca Dialogues and Essays.* Oxford: Oxford University Press.

De Seta, C. (1996). Grand tour: the lure of Italy in the eighteenth century. In Wilton, A. & Bignamini, I. (Eds.) *Grand tour: the lure of Italy in the eighteenth century.* London: Tate Gallery Publishing.

Elsner, J. & Rutherford, I. (2005). *Pilgrimage in Graeco-Roman and early Christian antiquity: seeing the gods.* Oxford: Oxford University Press.

Feifer, M. (1985). *Going Places: The Ways of the Tourist from Imperial Rome to the Present Day.* London: Macmillan.

Gerolemeu, M. (Ed.) (2018). *Recognising Miracles in Antiquity and Beyond.* Berlin/Boston: De Gruyter.

Gerritsen, A. (2007). *Ji'an literati and the local in Song-Yuan-Ming China.* Leiden: Brill.

Hargett, J. (1989). *On the road in twelfth century China: the travel diaries of Fan Chengda (1126–1193).* Stuttgart: Steiner Verlag Wiesbaden.

Heiss, H. (2002). Ownership of public houses by the Swiss nobility: a regional case-study. In Kümin, B.A. & Tlusty, B.A. (Eds.) *The world of the tavern: public houses in early modern Europe.* Aldershot; Burlington, VT: Ashgate.

Hemingway, E. (1964). *A moveable feast.* New York: Scribner.

Howard, P. (2003). *Heritage: management, interpretation, identity.* London: Continuum.

Jansen-Verbeke, M. & McKercher, B. (2010) The tourism destiny of world heritage cultural sites. In Pearce, D.G. & Butler, R.W. (Eds.) *Tourism research: a 20:20 vision.* Oxford: Goodfellow Publishers.

Keys, D. (2010, 29 September). Stonehenge a monumental attraction since prehistory. *The Independent.* https://www.independent.co.uk/news/science/stonehenge-a-monumental-attraction-since-prehistory-2092536.html.

Lassels, R. (1670). *The Voyage of Italy, or a Compleat Journey through Italy.* London: John Starkey.

Leed, E.J. (1991). *The mind of the traveller: from Gilgamesh to global tourism*. New York: Basic Books.

Lickorish, L. & Jenkins, C. (1997). *An introduction to tourism*. Oxford, Boston: Butterworth-Heinemann.

Lufrano, R. (1997). *Honorable merchants: commerce and self-cultivation in late imperial China*. Honolulu: University of Hawaii Press.

MacCannell, D. (1989). *The tourist*. London: Macmillan.

Mair, V. (Ed.). (1994). *The Columbia anthology of traditional Chinese literature*. New York: Columbia University Press.

McKercher, B. & du Cros, H. (2002). *Cultural tourism: the partnership between tourism and cultural heritage management*. New York: Routledge.

Naquin, S. & Rawski, E. (1987). *Chinese society in the eighteenth century*. New Haven, CT: Yale University Press.

Park, E. & Choi, B. (2011). Attractiveness of Gyeongbok Palace as a cultural heritage site. In Kozak, M. & Kozak, N. (Eds.) *Sustainability of tourism: cultural and environmental perspectives*. Newcastle upon Tyne: Cambridge Scholars Publishing.

Perdue, P. (2005). *China marches west: the Qing conquest of Central Eurasia*. Cambridge, MA: Belknap Press of Harvard University Press.

Pirie, G. (2004). Passenger traffic in the 1930s on British imperial air routes: refinement and revision. *Journal of Transport History*, 25(1), 63–83.

Richards, G. (Ed.). (2007). *Cultural tourism: global and local perspectives*. New York: Haworth Hospitality Press.

Schultz, P. (2011). *1000 places to see before you die*. New York: Workman.

Smith, M. (2009). *Issues in cultural tourism studies*. London: Routledge.

Swatos, W.H. & Tomasi, L. (2002). *From medieval pilgrimage to religious tourism: the social and cultural economics of piety*. Westport: Praeger.

Timothy, D.J. (2011). *Cultural and heritage tourism*. Bristol: Channel View.

Timothy, D.J. & Boyd, S.W. (2003). *Heritage tourism*. Harlow: Pearson Education.

Towner, J. (1985). The Grand Tour: a key phase in the history of tourism. *Annals of Tourism Research*, 12(3), 297–333.

Tribe, J. (1997). The indiscipline of tourism. *Annals of tourism research*, 24(3), 638–657.

Urry, J. (1990). *The tourist gaze*. London: SAGE.

VisitBritain (2016). Leveraging Britain's culture in Brazil, China & Italy. *Foresight* Issue 145.

Waterton, E. & Watson, S. (2010). *Culture, heritage and representation: perspectives on visuality and the past*. FarnhamAshgate.

Williams, C. (1998). *Travel culture: what makes us go*. Westport: Praeger.

Williams, W. (Ed.) (1992). *A Book of English Essays*. London: Penguin Books.

Williams, R. (1958). *Culture and society*. London: Chatto & Windus.

Winter, T., Teo, P. & Chang, T. (2009). *Asia on tour: exploring the rise of Asian Tourism*. London; New York: Routledge.

Wolmar, C. (2009). *Blood, iron & gold: how the railways transformed the world*. London: Atlantic Books.

Yan, L.B. (2010). *The contribution of early medieval china (AD 220–589) to the travel culture of landscape appreciation.* PhD thesis, Hong Kong Polytechnic University.

Zhang, C. (2011). *Transformative journeys: travel and culture in Song China.* Honolulu: University of Hawaii Press.

Zuelow, E. (2016). *A history of modern tourism.* London: Palgrave.

Further reading

Timothy, D.J. & Boyd, S.W. (2003). *Heritage tourism.* Harlow: Pearson Education.

Zuelow, E. (2016). *A history of modern tourism.* London: Palgrave.

3 Museums as tourism attractions

What is a museum experience?

Traditionally, museums have been repositories of artefacts to be cared for by skilled staff or curators. Increasingly they have become seen as guardians of collective memory and heritage, projectors of soft power and tourist attractions in their own right. Consequently, cultural heritage attractions are subject to the same vagaries identified by tourism theory that apply to other types of destination such as host-destination models (Mill and Morrison, 1985, Hall, 1995, Leiper, 1995), motivation (Richards, 2002), distance decay (Beaman, 1974, Bull, 1991, McKercher, 1998, McKercher and Lew, 2003), market access (McKercher, 1998), tourist behaviour (Lew and McKercher, 2006, Moutinho, 2001), finite time budgets (McKean, Johnson & Walsh, 1995) and destination lifecycles (Butler, 1980, Plog, 2001). However, one rarely sees such tourism theories applied specifically to museums as tourism attractions.

What is the point of a museum-like tourism experience? What is its purpose? To convey information? A book can do that in much greater depth. Provide some form of interactivity? The internet does that to your heart's content. Immersion? Something approaching that can be achieved with VR. So, it must provide something that a book, computer or mobile phone cannot. It must give the visitor a memorable, social experience that allows them to feel they have connected with something authentic. However, too often in the past museum spaces have been just filled with graphics:

> The visitor is standing on tired feet. The crowd is milling around. He's not used to reading at more than a 10-inch focus and certainly not in a vertical plane. He will skip the reading, it looks dull anyway. He concentrates on a small diagram, glances at a photograph, reads a caption or two and walks blissfully past the clinching

DOI: 10.4324/9781003369240-5

argument. Unless he is interested in typography the exhibition is not for him.

Gardner and Heller (1960)

This is a well-expressed indictment of the "books on wall" approach to museum exhibitions, which is the all-too-common fallback position of so many institutions; if you cannot come up with an effective exhibit then simply plaster the walls with text. The rule of thumb should be: if you cannot come up with an effective exhibit perhaps this topic does not warrant one. Even though the main visitation numbers of most museums are made up of school students, exhibitions should not simply be a physical manifestation of the classroom; they are something different. So, what are they?

Exhibitions are social spaces that inspire through storytelling and display. Stories have always been the main way that human beings have passed on information. Moreover, and this is particularly relevant for heritage-based exhibitions, "narrative is the principal way in which our species organises its understanding of time" (Abbott, 2005). Different phrases are used, sometimes inaccurately, to refer to this specialist sector which includes exhibition design, themed design, themed environments, experience design, immersive design, (the dreaded) "edutainment" and so on. My preferred terms are narrative or museum design which cover almost any creative output which is content- or storyline-driven with the aim of being informative and entertaining. This might, for instance, also include museum-like design techniques applied to non-museum environments such as retail or hospitality spaces.

There are a wide variety of museums which a designer might get involved with, each with subtly different expectations and approaches. Perhaps the first type of museum that people think of are those to do with history. These tend to be arranged by narratives according to chronology and topic, often as a linear pathway punctuated by moments of experience conveyed through objects, graphics, audiovisual and increasingly high-tech interactives. At the other end of the scale are science centres which tend to be arranged by topic and are highly interactive, often with few or no artefacts. The exhibits are often trying to convey ideas or phenomena that we might not be able to see ordinarily. They tend to emphasise "doing" in order to learn and can use the full gamut of interactivity, motion, experimentation (including demonstration) and sensory techniques. Although there is a wide-ranging "catalogue" of standard science museum exhibits now, bespoke exhibits may need to be devised by the designer which will require them to grapple with complex content and intensively prototype exhibits that may be subject to some rough handling by visitors of all ages.

Different again are art museums. These tend to be the most passive of visitor experiences, providing you with the opportunity to contemplate and learn about works of art, sculpture and multimedia installations in aesthetically conducive atmospheres. Certainly not places for quiet contemplation are children's museums. Every aspect of these facilities is focused on activity and interaction to convey simple principles about science and society at an educational level appropriate for kids. Visitor centres can include corporate museums, conservation parks and heritage centres, public information centres and so on, and tend to be focused on a narrower set of messaging objectives with a less universal and more directed mission. They may be part of a specific local, regional or national campaign to raise awareness about a particular issue such as drug addiction or habitat loss. Park visitor centres may have the challenge of dealing with the interpretation of extensive outdoor landscapes and wildlife. They might address a very wide audience, such as the general public, or a very specific audience, such as corporate staff and VIPs. They often use the full range of museum display techniques, but corporate museum exhibits may not need the same level of "child-proofing" if the general public is not the target audience.

The development of museums as attractions

When does demand for museum or heritage attractions become an economic or social imperative? According to Brokensha & Guldberg (1992), some of the prerequisites are an increasing awareness of heritage, an ability to express individuality, greater economic affluence, increased leisure time, mobility, access to the arts and the need to seek transcendent experiences. An attraction might be something that has evolved quite organically, such as Cantonese cuisine, but the deliberate creation of attractions enables a more controlled approach to dealing with mass tourism. This can help minimise the impact to the host community and maximise the experience for the tourists, as well as the returns to be potentially ploughed into sustainable practices. The more mainstream the target audience, the more controlled the experience needs to be (McKercher & du Cros, 2002). We must of course also be careful that we are aware of our characterisation of the tourist as an "all-encompassing, analytical monolith" (Winter, Teo & Chang, 2009), in other words a white, Western male. The weight of academic tourism history from North American and European institutions can sometimes blind us to the local and regional tourists at the doors of our very own attractions.

There are many types of heritage tourism attractions. Timothy (2011) divides his list of sample attractions into two broad categories – tangible and intangible (Figure 3.1).

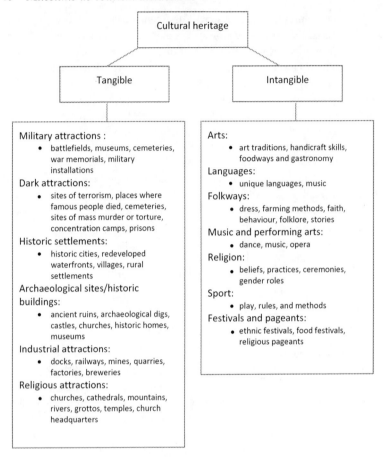

Figure 3.1 Timothy's heritage attractions categories

As we saw in Chapter 2, there are three main classes of heritage assets: buildings and archaeological sites; heritage cities, routes and cultural landscapes; and movable cultural property and museums. And from an attraction-driven visitor perspective, types of heritage tourism might be broken down into genres of artistic, natural, living cultural, built, industrial, personal or dark, military or literary heritage. On the grand scale, the institutional version of the heritage bucket list is UNESCO's world heritage site list that currently comprises 1,154 properties – natural (218), cultural (897) and mixed (39) – of "outstanding universal value". This listing, requiring as it does the practices of surveying, recording, documentation and conservation by experts, confers upon these sites a symbolic or cultural capital which, if suitably treated and manipulated, can be converted and commodified into economic value (Bandelj and Wherry, 2011). The amenability to "cultural capitalisation" means that heritage can certainly be packaged as a tourism product.

Figure 3.2 Italy (58) currently outranks China (56) as the country with the most UNESCO World Heritage Sites, with the archaeological site at the ruins of Pompeii being one of the most visited
Source: Photograph by Victor Malyushev on Unsplash.

Indeed, not recognising heritage assets as the tourism products they are can lead to a failure to optimise their benefit or, in other words, exploit them properly.

In the 1980s and particularly the 1990s, the museum world in the UK and the United States (US) began to realise that the objects on display in national collections were only talking to aficionados. Too many people were not seeing themselves reflected in the "powerful mirror" of their own heritage. These debates about representation, ownership and access have important implications for their distant cousin the heritage tourism product. In other words, who's telling the story, whose story are we telling and to whom are we telling it? Vergo (1989) identified the root of the problem as being too much discussion about museum methods and not enough about the purposes of museums.

The key trend in 1980s Britain was a Thatcherite-led reduction in public funding which forced museums to find other sources of income such as corporate sponsorship and, increasingly, charging visitors for entry, particularly for special exhibitions. This commercialisation of museums meant that they had to reinvent themselves as entertainment commodities in an experience economy. Critics derided the dumbing down of museums and the perceived requirement for them to compete with theme parks. Throughout the 1980s and 90s, the purpose of museums was being increasingly redefined by both the people who held the private purse strings and their potential audiences. The shift from an object-based curatorial-focused approach to a more visitor-centric philosophy meant that new methods of developing museums were needed. And this was not just a UK, US or even European phenomenon; rising economies such as Taiwan embarked on ambitious programmes of museum building. Many of these new museums had no objects at all (being about science or natural science) and so enhanced techniques of storytelling, interpretive planning and designing for museums evolved. As few museums had their own design departments (or in the case of new museums often lacked even a curatorial team), this emerging aspect of the experience economy gave rise to a new wave of creative professionals in the niche specialist three-dimensional interior design category of museum design.

In the UK, this process was only accelerated by money made available for large-scale visitor centres around the country by the Lottery Fund through the Millennium Commission on a variety of topics from pop music to digital art. The high point (or nadir depending on your viewpoint) was the Millennium Dome which, despite overwhelmingly negative media coverage, was surprisingly well visited. Not all of these projects were a success for a wide range of reasons. Half the battle for these institutions was to actually realise that they were a tourism product; failure to understand this in heritage tourism development leads to a lack of understanding of market demand, asset evaluation, clearly defined management objectives and priorities and the isolation of product development (Ho & McKercher, 2008). "Presentation, interpretation and verification has a direct bearing on motivations to visit and engage with heritage tourism sites" (Bryce et al., 2015).

The need for authenticity

Whatever the type of cultural or heritage attraction, they all need to embody or contain some form of authenticity, whether that be in terms of location, artefact or experience, to be successful. One of the perceived weaknesses of the Millennium Dome was its overblown, artificial nature. However, an attraction as seemingly fanciful as the Harry Potter experience at the Warner Bros. Studio in the UK can assume an air of authenticity by genuinely being the place where so many of the scenes from the films were made. Since the 1960s, debates around authenticity have revolved around the degree to which visitors are seeking it (Boorstin, 1964) and to what extent they are knowingly or unknowingly complicit in a process of staged authenticity (Cohen, 1988, MacCannell, 1973, 1989). There is a lack of consensus within the literature about what constitutes authenticity but three major strands emerge: objective, constructive and existential.

Objective approaches place the authenticity of the object of the tourist gaze as an essential component to the activity and experience (Cohen, 1979). The acceptance of an ideal of uniqueness or originality leads to the possibility of the observer being somehow duped or misled. MacCannell (1973), in particular, is the prime prosecutor of the destination tourism industry's crime of foisting a version of staged authenticity on an unsuspecting public. The cultural fare (performances, displays, museums, guides, site interpretation, etc.) placed in front of tourist audiences are often maligned as being unrepresentative, ersatz and possibly demeaning to the host community (Boorstin, 1964). But in many ways this approach draws on a purist tradition going back to Ruskin's 19th-century Romanticism which prioritised the cultural experience over the Thomas Cook-ian democratisation of travel and made the quality of the artefacts, monuments and natural scenes matter intensely, giving them moral and political urgency (Hanley & Walton, 2010).

Cohen (1988) and Urry (1990) give the tourist the benefit of the doubt that they might at least have some powers of analytical thought, irony, humour, insight and ability to see things from multiple perspectives.

This constructivist approach sees authenticity to be something that has a socio-cultural origin that can be built by the observer almost knowingly. Inevitably, on any particular visit, tourism products provide strong influences in terms of how this sense of authenticity might be constructed, with interpretation at the heart of it.

There seems to be a tension between globalisation and authenticity that reflects a focus on the effects of the actualisation, commercialisation and commodification of the object of the cultural tourists' gaze (Richards, 2007, McKercher & du Cros, 2002). The need to cater for a mass audience from a wide range of nations might be seen to inevitably to lead to a "dumbing down" of content. It is an accusation that has been levelled at cultural products from the belly dance to the British Museum. But might this be less of a reflection on the audience and more of an underestimation by the commentators of their audiences' intellectual or aesthetic capacity? Chhabra, Healy and Sills (2003) argue, however, that this does not totally negate all authenticity as "what is staged is not superficial since it contains elements of the original tradition". Indeed, how long does an object or event have to be in existence to achieve heritage status and so a sense of authenticity?

This leads us to the idea that authenticity is actually divorced from the object itself and acts on the observer as a way of defining the self (Wang, 1999). This existential authenticity is activated by the tourist experience or in other words the tourist experience acts as a catalyst (Brown, 2013) even if the toured objects are inauthentic. It has been argued, therefore, that the perception of authenticity is almost as real an experience for tourists as touching an original artefact with an accurate provenance.

In our post-structuralist, pleasure-seeking world, tourists and indeed curators of cultural tourism are seen as negotiating their way through the images and experiences presented to them constructing their own reality. Chhabra (2008) posits a negotiation model (Figure 3.3) as part of a continuum on which museum curators pick a path between the traditional roles of research and conservation (essentialist) and interpretive staging (constructivist) of authenticity, taking into account their increasingly complex institutional missions and donor/sponsor concerns, to create positive outcomes of creating social capital and a sense of activism in their diverse audiences.

When considering visitor attractions, there is the added dimension of trying to elicit an emotional response from visitors to events that might be historically or culturally distant for which the evidence may be a faint outline of brickwork on the ground (in the case of an archaeological site, for instance). Where verifiably authentic objects exist for display

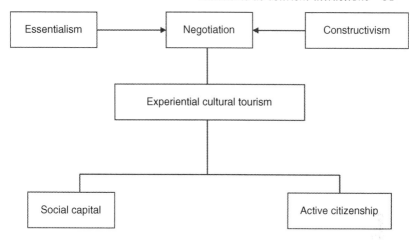

Figure 3.3 Chhabra's Negotiation Model

purposes, they may be boringly everyday objects or in poor condition. This might tempt the commissioners of the visitor attraction to create some form of audiovisual extravaganza, but this immediately opens itself to the accusation of being inauthentic. The curators, interpreters and designers may all themselves have no first-hand knowledge of the theme of the attraction (many industrial open-air museums do well to use volunteers from the site's former industry as guides). So in trying to enable visitors to grasp authentic emotions of, for instance, a historical site of trauma, one is reminded of the lyrics of Pulp's song 'Common People' when a shameless class tourist is trying get a taste of working-class life without enduring its true hardships:

> 'Cos everybody hates a tourist
> Especially one who thinks it's all such a laugh
> Yeah and the chip stain and grease will come out in the bath
> You will never understand
> How it feels to live your life
> With no meaning or control
> And with nowhere left to go
> You are amazed that they exist
> And they burn so bright whilst you can only wonder why.

Cohen and Cohen (2012) begin to address the range of authentications (from cool to hot) within the tourist attraction sector which means that differentiated offers of personal authenticity can be provided and understood. Cool authentication tends towards objective authenticity or museumisation and hot towards constant re-enactment and experiential authenticity. But it is also arguable that all three aspects of authenticity (objective, constructive and existential) are often commonly present (indeed demanded by the visiting audience) in some form in most museum, visitor attraction or heritage tourism experiences. Certainly, good interpretive planning will usually attempt to cater for or encompass all of these aspects of authenticity. Interpretations collide and cross-pollinate, and there seems to be a knowingness to the tourists' use of the product that makes authenticity only one success criteria for the experience. A post-modern, pluralist society with a habit of civic (and civil) discourse between competing sectors (government, academic, commercial, NGOs, hobbyists, etc.) demands a product that is open-ended and accommodating of a variety of viewpoints. Introducing competing voices into the museum or attraction is a way of bolstering a sense of authenticity.

Figure 3.4 Even though The Making of Harry Potter experience is completely fabricated it is authentically the place where the films were made
Source: Photograph by Chris White.

Heritage attractions and urban revitalisation

In tourism terms, cities represent a concentration of tangible urban structures that can usually be regarded as historically significant. Ask any primary school child to tell you what they know about a great world city and it will probably be some form of heritage tourism that they enthuse about – the Eiffel Tower or the changing of the guard at Buckingham Palace. Second-tier cities or districts of established world cities can use the revitalisation of an area or particular heritage asset as a means of attracting more tourists.

There are many words used for breathing new life into urban areas – regeneration, revitalisation, renaissance – but they all imply that there was some form of energy (industrial, economic or creative) that has gone into decline and requires reinvigorating. This deindustrialisation/regeneration phenomenon often goes hand-in-hand with a desire to conserve the hardware (infrastructure, buildings, etc.) of an area whilst plugging in new software (culture, arts, recreation, etc.) through an adaptive re-use approach. The emerging experience sector in the 1990s, coupled with government policies particularly in Europe, prompted the use of urban spaces as stages on which experiential events can take place (Richards, 2001). This "festivalisation" usually has an economic motive in trying to bring new sources of income to a depressed area and so its success is often measured in terms of employment creation, multiplier effects and visitor expenditure. More recently, community involvement and development have become an important indicator of success in such projects. The complex impulses and desired outcomes of such projects are represented by Smith (2009) in Table 3.1.

Any or all of these aspects and outcomes can co-exist in a single project; urban regeneration projects are amongst the most complex capital

Table 3.1 Overview of different aspects and outcomes of regeneration

Regeneration as ...				
a 'panacea' for economic decline	a tool for social development	physical improvement	aestheticisation or beautification	a political or image-enhancing tool
Job creation Attraction of investment Tourism development	Housing Education Entertainment	Conservation Environmental protection Renovation	Landscaping Public art Animation	Flagship buildings Mega-events Branding

Source: Smith (2009).

projects it is possible to undertake. Looking back at Timothy's heritage
attraction categories (Figure 3.1), some heritage assets lend themselves
more readily to adaptive re-use than others. Two aspects of this are
worthy of comment from the point of view of urban revitalisation and
interpretation. Firstly, revitalisation usually involves adaptive re-use
that might include retail and restaurants. Under the 'Tangible' column,
certain types of attraction immediately suggest themselves as more
suitable for being at the heart of revitalisation projects (historic settle-
ments, for instance) than others (dark attractions, for example). Secondly, the 'Intangible' column can act upon the 'Tangible' through the
process of interpretation to materially affect the experience found
within these tangible cultural assets. When thinking about the diagram
in this way, it becomes clear that history must be included in this
column as well. So, in looking at types of attraction from the point of
view of interpretation within types of heritage attractions, one could
amend this table as follows:

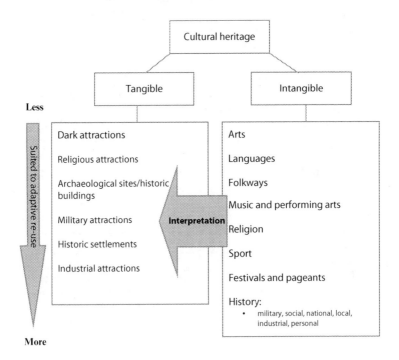

Figure 3.5 Amended heritage attractions categories

Whilst culture may on the face of it often be the primary motive in "cultural regeneration" projects, they tend to take an instrumental approach to enable more quantitative political and economic outcomes. Along the way, this tends to push aside the more intangible or qualitative aspects of culture that may be important to local people, such as a sense of place, identity, personal histories and so on.

The fabric of a city can be interpreted in a number of ways: museums and study centres, trails and walks and location markers (such as public art). Across all the tangible attractions, the most common vehicle for communicating information or an experience of the site is some form of museum – whether that be purpose-built, integrated into existing architectural fabric or open-air. A museum-like experience for the visitor might range from a very small museum consisting of graphic panels and some artefacts, to an immersive audiovisual experience, to an outdoor trail. Most visitor centres incorporate museum-like exhibition techniques and often act as an essential anchor to a range of offers, providing a convenient location for practical visitor facilities such as information desks, toilets, souvenir shops and staff offices.

However, sometimes the balance between heritage and commercial regeneration can go badly wrong. Built in 1884, the compound of buildings that was the Hong Kong Marine Police Headquarters in Tsim Sha Tsui was declared a monument in 1994. In 2002, Hong Kong's parliament or Legislative Council (LegCo) agreed to preserve, restore and convert it for tourism-related uses. The rationale for this was as follows:

> There has been increasing public demand for more to be done to preserve our heritage assets. Given budgetary and other constraints on Government, there is a strong case for a new approach to preserve and exploit these facilities. One of the most suitable ways to do this is to engage private sector resources in suitable projects with commercial potential. This will help inject new ideas and a new dynamism into the process to convert our heritage assets to beneficial use. This will also enable Government to focus its resources on preservation work which does not offer a potential for private sector participation.
>
> (Hong Kong LegCo, File Ref: ESB CR 22/24/17)

The stated intention was to develop the site as a "heritage tourism facility." In May 2003, the Hong Kong government awarded the tender for redevelopment on a 50-year land grant at HK$352.8 million. However, both during its development and after its opening in August 2009, the project was dogged by controversy. Conservationists' concerns included a large numbers of trees (149 of the original) lost and some century-old trees transplanted into inadequate pots out of context with the original site, the loss of the topography of Tsim Sha Tsui Hill and a failure to accurately measure the exact floor size of the historic buildings (resulting in a 30 per cent gain for the developer that was discovered after the handover and opening of the site). More strikingly, the overall effect of the end result is one of a highly-commercialised site with little obvious attempt to tell its story, festooned with brand signage with little sense of the original ambience of the site.

The Guggenheim Museum in Bilbao is the darling of the cultural regeneration movement. With all due respect to the city, what other reason could one think of for visiting as a tourist this northern Spanish city that had been in decline due to deindustrialisation and terrorism since the 1980s? As the core attraction of a regeneration effort, the "Bilbao effect" saw it consistently contribute approximately a million visitors to the city from its opening in 1997 (Plaza & Haarich, 2015). It is a model that many aspirational second- or third-tier cities around the world seek to replicate (just as so many Chinese cities want their own Lan Kwai Fong or *Xintiandi*). It should be remembered, however, that short city breaks in Europe have become a tourism phenomenon in themselves that may pose a serious threat to both the sustainability and heritage fabric of a number of historic towns. Heritage tourism to small historic city centres exemplify the fine balance between conservation and visitor management. Plaza and Haarich (2015) point out that it is not enough to simply build an institution like the Guggenheim "and they will come"; ongoing work on embedding the museum locally and regionally as well as growing its global networking is necessary. The common punchbag of the cultural regeneration movement is the UK's Millennium Dome in Greenwich, South London. This is mainly due to the ballooning costs (more than £800 million) and negative press associated with it. However, the fact remains that the visitor numbers of over 6.5 million to the Millennium Dome in the year 2000 was the largest number of visitors to any UK attraction in half a century and it was the most popular visitor attraction in Europe that year.

Two regions of significant growth for museums as tourism attractions in the first two decades of the 21st century are China and the Middle East. The adoption of the UNESCO Convention on the Protection of Natural and Cultural Heritage in 1985 appears to have fuelled an initial China museum boom, with numbers growing from around 400 in 1980 to over 1,200 in 1996. By 2015, this number had grown to over 3,800, at a rate of around 300 per year since 2005, with museum expenditure outstripping general cultural capital expenditure over that nearly 20-year period. Not only has the number count of museums tripled between 1996 and 2015, but the size and quality of museums have increased, with total museum space increasing by a factor of six and total expenditure by a

Figure 3.6 The Guggenheim Bilbao is a powerful tourist draw, attracting between 500,000 and 1 million visitors per year to a city of only 350,000 inhabitants
Source: Photograph by David Vives on Unsplash.

factor of sixteen. Zhang and Courty (2020) found that over this period China created a few high budget "superstar" museums managed centrally and many small and low-budget museums managed locally, with an increase in the average size and expenditure of all museums. By the end of 2020, the total number of museums in China had surged to 5,788, an increase of 23 per cent compared to 2015. In terms of the purposes of these new museums, Varutti (2014) finds that they have a primary intention to consolidate a sense of identity through a narrative around the longevity and continuity of the Chinese nation (much as happened in 19th-and 20th-century European museums). There has been widespread "museumification" of a range of tourism attractions, from high-end public art galleries to private patriotic collections to whole villages presenting ethnographic living museums (Graburn & Lu, 2017).

In parallel with this latter period of development, the Gulf States have become a new epicentre of museum development. The arrival of the Louvre Abu Dhabi in 2007 heralded a new era of Middle Eastern mega-museum that has seen the opening of the Museum of Islamic Art in 2008 and Mathaf: the Arab Museum of Modern Art in 2010 in Doha, a major cultural district on Abu Dhabi's Saadiyet Island containing several large museums, the acclaimed National Museum of Qatar in 2016 and the

Museum of the Future in 2022 in Dubai. The largest of the Guggenheim art museums is planned to open in the next few years in Abu Dhabi and Saudi Arabia has embarked on an ambitious plan to develop dozens of major new museums by 2030 creating more than 100,000 new jobs in the kingdom. All of the museums mentioned are major tourist attractions in their own right for the region and internationally. It would seem that the role of museums as drivers of the tourism economy is alive and well in the 21st century.

Box 3.1 Case study 3: The National Museum of Qatar

As with many economies around the world heavily reliant on fossil fuels, Qatar as a nation has been seeking to diversify its source of income. Tourism is seen as a key component of the economy going forward. Between 2020 and 2030 tourism is expected to add over 100,000 jobs and contribute over US$20.3bn to the nation's GDP. And at the heart of the promotion of tourism is renewed focus on its seven major museums which includes the 40,000 square-metre National Museum of Qatar, opened in March 2019. This is very much a country in search of a nationwide "Bilbao effect" through this signature piece of cultural investment (in the region of US$434 million for the building alone). Designed by Jean Nouvel, the facade of the museum building features curved discs representing crystal clusters found in the Qatari desert known as desert roses.

Inside, the museum has 11 interlocking galleries (including Sheikh Abdullah bin Jassim Al Thani's original palace) forming a continuous narrative that interprets Qatar's human and natural history from ancient to modern times, divided into three chapters: Beginnings, Life in Qatar and the Modern History of Qatar. According to Jean Nouvel (2022)

> The building I designed needed to reflect these three different stories. The first, which covers a long period, is the story of the peninsula and its inhabitants. The second is an exploration of the coastal and desert lifestyles as well as the pearling industry, and third covers the spectacular acceleration that gave the kingdom – in just a few decades – the power and prosperity we associate with it today. Because of its economic power, Qatar has become a world leader in fields as diverse as education, communications, and energy technology. The desert rose, a flower-like aggregate of mineral crystals occurring only in arid coastal regions, is the first architectural structure that nature itself creates, through wind, sea spray and sand acting together over millennia. It's surprisingly complex and poetic.

Figure 3.7 The National Museum of Qatar welcomed more than 450,000 visitors in its first year of opening in 2019 and was named in *TIME* magazine's list of the "World's Greatest Places to Visit" in the same year

Source: Photograph by Jirayu Koontholjinda on Unsplash.

The museum's first gallery ("The Formation of Qatar") begins the story more than 700 million years ago, when powerful geological forces shaped the peninsula and was home to now extinct land and sea creatures. This first gallery features a film by Christophe Cheysson ("The Beginnings"). Central displays present fossils of animals and plants from seven time periods, with an interactive exhibit allowing in-depth exploration of the complex geological processes that created the Qatari peninsula. The second gallery ("Qatar's Natural Environment") focuses on the adaptation of the country's flora and fauna to their habitats with models of Qatar's land and sea creatures for visitors to explore the interconnection between different species and environments to understand the fragility of Qatar's ecosystems. In "The Archaeology of Qatar" visitors discover the story of the people of Qatar through approximately 1,000 archaeological artefacts, which are displayed in glass cases to form an extended chronology, as well as reconstructions of ancient burial sites and a family-friendly, hands-on excavation site.

The first gallery of the second chapter ("Life in Qatar") is "The People of Qatar" which begins with an exploration of movement as a fundamental element in the identity of the Qatari people: seasonal movement between *al barr* (the inland desert) and the coast; movement to find water and pastures; and movement to buy and sell goods. The "Life in Al Barr" gallery expresses how living in the harsh environment of the desert draws communities together through poetry, song and woven textiles. The next gallery, "Life on the Coast", provides a large-scale model of the archaeological site of Al Zubarah, Qatar's first UNESCO World Heritage listing. The "Pearls and Celebrations" gallery showcases the beauty of pearls harvested in the waters of Qatar through displays of costumes, jewellery and musical instruments.

The final chapter of the nation's narrative begins with "Building the Nation" that presents the political history of Qatar between 1500 and 1913. An art film by Peter Webber evokes the final battle before unification, while the sounds and smells of warfare draw you into the gallery, past beautiful models of Portuguese, Ottoman, British and Qatari ships. Objects on display include weapons and historic maps, items related to significant battles and personal possessions of the leaders of Qatar. The "Industry and Innovation" gallery explains how the collapse of the pearling industry and the discovery of oil has led to a rejuvenated, engineering-based economy. The final gallery, "Qatar Today", uses immersive digital technology to dramatically narrate Qatar in the reign of the current emir, HH Sheikh Tamim bin Hamad Al Thani. The design of the galleries is James Gardner-esque (see Chapter 7) with grand, sweeping environmental and contextual audiovisual backdrops to beautifully crafted focal exhibits. Testament to its iconic attraction and successful promotion, the museum welcomed more than 132,000 visitors in its first month.

Conclusion

The role of museums has changed from simple repositories and curators of objects to full-blown cultural tourism attractions. This has led to diversification in types of museums, how they address their audiences, how they are developed and expectations as to how they will contribute to local, regional and national economies. In some cases, museums and heritage tourism sites have become flagships for regenerating whole cities and even countries. The development and understanding of the museum's role as a tourist attraction has spread into large new markets such as the Middle East and presents opportunities for government advisors and commercial consultants to get involved, positively contributing to economies, cultural enrichment and new experiences for visitors.

References

Abbott, H. (2005). *The Cambridge introduction to narrative*. Cambridge: Cambridge University Press.

Bandelj, N. & Wherry, F. (Eds.). (2011). *The cultural wealth of nations*. Stanford, CA: Stanford University Press.

Beaman, J. (1974). Distance and the reaction to distance as a function of distance. *Journal of Leisure Research*, 6(Summer), 220–231.

Boorstin, D. (1964). *The image: a guide to pseudo-events in America*. New York: Harper.

Brokensha, P. & Guldberg, H. (1992). *Cultural tourism in Australia: a report on cultural tourism*. Canberra: Australian Government Publishing Service.

Brown, L. (2013). Tourism: a catalyst for existential authenticity. *Annals of Tourism Research*, 40(1), 176–190.

Bryce, D., Curran, R., O'Gorman, K. & Taheri, B. (2015). Visitors' engagement and authenticity: Japanese heritage consumption. *Tourism Management*, 46, 571–581.

Bull, A. (1991). *The economics of travel and tourism*. Melbourne: Pitman.

Butler, R.W. (1980). The concept of tourism area cycle of evolution: the implications for management of resources. *The Canadian Geographer*, 24, 5–12.

Chhabra, D., Healy, R. & Sills, E. (2003). Staged authenticity and heritage tourism. *Annals of Tourism Research*, 30(3), 702–719.

Chhabra, D. (2008). Positioning museums on an authenticity continuum. *Annals of Tourism Research*, 35(2), 427–447.

Cohen, E. (1979). A phenomenology of tourist experience. *Sociology*, 13, 179–201.

Cohen, E. (1988). Authenticity and commoditization in tourism. *Annals of Tourism Research*, 15(3), 371–386.

Cohen, E. & Cohen, S. (2012). Authentication: hot and cool. *Annals of Tourism Research*, 39(3), 1295–1314.

Gardner, J. & Heller, C. (1960). *Exhibition and display*. London: Batsford.

Graburn, N. & Lu, J. (2017). Tourism and museums in China. *Asian Journal of Tourism Research*, 2(1), 1–34.

Hall, M. (1995) *Introduction to Tourism*. 2nd Edition. Melbourne: Longman.

Hanley, K. & Walton, J.K. (2010). *Constructing cultural tourism: John Ruskin and the tourist gaze*. Bristol: Channel View Publications.

Ho, P. & McKercher, B. (2008). Managing heritage resources as tourism products. In Prideaux, B., Timothy, D. & Chon, K. (Eds.) *Cultural and heritage tourism in Asia and the Pacific*. London: Routledge.

Hong Kong LegCo, File Ref: ESB CR 22/24/17.

Leiper, N. (1995). *Tourism management*. Melbourne: RMIT Press.

Lew, A. & McKercher, B. (2006). Modeling tourist movement: a local destination analysis. *Annals of Tourism Research*, 33(2), 403–423.

MacCannell, D. (1973). Staged authenticity: arrangements of social space in tourist settings. *American Journal of Sociology*, 79(3), 589–603.

MacCannell, D. (1989). *The tourist*. London: Macmillan.

McKean, J., Johnson, D. & Walsh, R. (1995) Valuing time in travel cost demand analysis: an empirical investigation. *Land Economics*, 71(1), 96–105.

McKercher, B. (1998). The effect of market access on destination choice. *Journal of Travel Research*, 37(1), 39–47.

McKercher, B. (1998). The effect of distance decay on visitor mix at coastal destinations. *Pacific Tourism Review*, 2(3/4), 215–224.

McKercher, B. & du Cros, H. (2002). *Cultural tourism: the partnership between tourism and cultural heritage management*. New York: Routledge.

McKercher, B. & Lew, A. (2003). Distance decay and the impact of effective tourism exclusion zones on international travel flows. *Journal of Travel Research*, 42(2), 159–165.

Mill, R. & Morrison, A. (1985). *The tourism system: an introductory text*. Englewood Cliffs, NJ: Prentice Hall.

Moutinho, L. (2001). Consumer behaviour. *Tourism European Journal of Marketing*, 21(10), 5–44.

Nouvel, J. (2022). www.jeannouvel.com/en/projects/musee-national-du-qatar (last accessed 21 September 2022).

Plaza, B. & Haarich, S. (2015). The Guggenheim Museum Bilbao: between regional embeddedness and global networking. *European Planning Studies*, 23(8), 1–20.

Plog, S. (2001). Why destination areas rise and fall in popularity: an update of a Cornell Quarterly Classic. *Cornell Hotel and Restaurant Quarterly*, 42(3), 13–24.

Richards, G. (Ed.). (2001). *Cultural attractions and European tourism*. Wallingford; New York: CABIN Pub.

Richards, G. (2002). Tourism attraction systems: exploring cultural behaviour. *Annals of Tourism Research*, 29(4), 1048–1064.

Richards, G. (Ed.). (2007). *Cultural tourism: global and local perspectives*. New York: Haworth Hospitality Press.

Smith, M. (2009). *Issues in cultural tourism studies*. London; New York: Routledge.

Timothy, D. (2011). *Cultural and heritage tourism*. Bristol; Ontario; New York: Channel View.

Urry, J. (1990). *The tourist gaze*. London: SAGE.

Varutti, M. (2014). *Museums in China: the politics of representation after Mao*. Woodbridge: Boydell Press.

Vergo, P. (1989). *The new museology*. London: Reaktion.

Wang, N. (1999). Rethinking authenticity in tourism experience. *Annals of Tourism Research*, 26(2), 349–370.

Winter, T., Teo, P. & Chang, T. (2009). *Asia on tour: exploring the rise of Asian Tourism*. London; New York: Routledge.

Zhang, F. & Courty, P. (2020). The China museum boom: soft power and cultural nationalism. *International Journal of Cultural Policy*: 27(5), 1–20.

Further reading

Corsane, G. (2005). *Heritage, museums and galleries: an introductory reader.* Abingdon: Routledge.

McKercher, B. & du Cros, H. (2002). *Cultural tourism: the partnership between tourism and cultural heritage management.* New York: Routledge.

Part II

Practice

Introduction

There are many practical sources of information on how to acquire, store and care for museum collections. Here we are looking at practical issues that might be encountered in museum-like projects for tourism by those who may not be professional curators. Who is our audience or audiences? Whose story are we telling and from what perspectives? What is that narrative and how do we evidence it? How are those aspirations for the project then implemented through the design process? What do we do when a major event such as a pandemic disrupts normal operations?

The role of interpretive planning has evolved from a niche service only offered within some commercial museum companies to being a product that sustains large companies in certain tourism-oriented markets. In this section, we look at the way issues around interpretation such as representation and authenticity impact on the process of planning heritage products for tourism, with a particular focus on the transformation of Hong Kong's decommissioned Central Police Station, Victoria Prison and Central Magistrates' Court into the Tai Kwun Centre for Heritage and the Arts which has attracted over ten million visitors in its first four years of operation.

Museum design specialists often encounter both public and private sector clients who have been put in the position of commissioning relatively large-scale, museum-like projects with no prior experience. A museum design process has been developing over the last 30 years with an increasing degree of consistency in terms of project planning and management. In the second chapter of this section, we look at lessons learned and best practices for implementing museum-like projects for tourism from inception to handover, including the make-up of the team, with a case study from one of the leaders in the field of specialist museum-project management.

DOI: 10.4324/9781003369240-6

Finally in this section, we live in an era of renewed awareness about our interconnectedness. This was particularly highlighted during the COVID-19 pandemic and we look at the relevant lessons learned for museums and tourism, with a reflection from the Old Royal Naval College, Greenwich.

4 Issues in interpretation

Visitors and audiences

Most projects in the museum or heritage sector start with a simple ambition: to tell a story. This might be through a site, a collection or a themed experience. However, this ambition is not as simple as it seems. As someone who is seeking to interpret a site, one may face a number of challenges from surprising sources. First of all, the client themselves (whilst paying lip service to the idea of general public access and story-telling) may unwittingly fall into the trap of addressing a narrow interest group (such as their senior management, corporate investors or elite connoisseurs). Secondly, designers (with whom you may be working to realise a project) sometimes design for other designers rather than the intended audience. One's role as the interpreter or interpretive planner is to represent the target audience(s) steadfastly and tenaciously, and usually this is the general public. If a subject matter expert is explaining something to you and you do not understand it, then it is likely that nor will most people, and you certainly will not be able to incorporate this information in any meaningful way in an exhibition or display. Understanding your audience and the content you wish to impart to them is the key to all interpretation.

Any cultural product – whether it be a book, film or theatre production – needs to be created with an audience in mind. Museums and exhibitions are no different in this regard. So, who are museums for? In the past, it was generally assumed to be a cultured, educated elite. In the post-war spirit of greater egalitarianism in Britain, for instance, it was generally accepted that museums are for everyone. However, "everyone" is not a homogenous group and over the years, as British demographics have changed through immigration and different minority groups have become increasingly empowered (such as the LGBTQ+ community), appealing to everyone is a more complex task. It is not simply a matter

DOI: 10.4324/9781003369240-7

of needing to appeal to all ages or backgrounds; it may be necessary to actively reach out through the interpretation to certain sections of the community to specifically engage them in the subject matter. Better still is to involve and incorporate those communities in the decision-making of the development process.

Museums put a lot of effort into trying to find out who visits them. Obviously, a huge section of visitation for any attraction, including museums, are school groups – effectively captive audiences. There is a close correlation between somebody's educational level and their like-lihood of visiting a museum. This may not simply be an outcome of education but also come down to things such as ways of socialising within certain social groups and to notions of what the French sociolo-gist Pierre Bourdieu termed "cultural capital". If we are to take London as an example, residents of the richest borough of Kensington and Chelsea have the highest uptake of free and state-subsidised cultural and arts offers, whilst the poorest boroughs have the lowest (Mason, Robin-son & Coffield, 2018). Despite the low cost of participation, there are obviously still barriers (cultural, social, environmental) to consumption.

Obviously, allied to studies of who visits are questions around why people visit. The notion that museums are places of useful information and education clearly ensures that an important part of a museum's visitor numbers (school students) keep coming back year after year. Education is also an important reason why governments around the world invest large amounts of public money in new museums. Back in the 1980s, this was evident in the programme of museum-building in Asian tiger economies such as Taiwan, in which I was involved. Many families also see a trip to a museum as a worthwhile activity, particularly on a rainy day. This means taking into account the needs of a range of age groups within the family, from babies to grandparents, as well as providing food, beverages and merchandising opportunities. If a museum is not providing the opportunity to address the needs of the whole family and entertain/educate them for a whole day, they are missing a trick. This is one way of looking at the dif-ferent segments of the museum's audience and how they can be catered for.

The role of interpretation

Tilden's six principles

> Through interpretation, understanding; through understanding, apprecia-tion; through appreciation, protection.
>
> 1950s US National Park Service manual as quoted by
> Freeman Tilden (1977)

Commonly, discussions about interpretation in tourism or museums begin with a reference to Freeman Tilden's six principles (Tilden, 1977) which were intended to reveal "something of the beauty and wonder, the inspiration and spiritual meaning that lie behind what the visitor can with his senses perceive":

1. Any interpretation that does not somehow relate what is being displayed or described to something within the personality or experience of the visitor will be sterile.
2. Information, as such, is not Interpretation. Interpretation is revelation based upon information. But they are entirely different things. However, all interpretation includes information.
3. Interpretation is an art, which combines many arts, whether the materials presented are scientific, historical or architectural. Any art is in some degree teachable.
4. The chief aim of Interpretation is not instruction, but provocation.
5. Interpretation should aim to present a whole rather than a part and must address itself to the whole man rather than any phase.
6. Interpretation addressed to children (say up to the age of 12) should not be a dilution of the presentation to adults but should follow a fundamentally different approach. To be at its best it will require a separate program.

Sometimes, Tilden's interpretive principles are reduced to three key elements – to relate, reveal and provoke. These principles have been built upon in the theory and practice of the last 50 years but fundamentally remain relevant. They reveal a clearly constructivist approach where interpreters of knowledge aim to provoke visitors to build their own understandings rather than simply to "teach" something. It should be remembered that these principles were formulated in the United States in the 1960s and were focused primarily on guided interpretation of national parks. Tilden has subsequently been criticised, perhaps not entirely fairly, by Staiff (2014) who argues that, rather than institutional gatekeepers revealing meaning intrinsically contained within objects to visitors, meaning is created by the visitor within a cultural and historical frame of reference. However, many institutions and attractions continue to didactically communicate information as a linear, deterministic series of objects.

Education and entertainment

There have traditionally been two main roles ascribed to interpretation – education and entertainment (Timothy, 2011). The educative role can be both formal in terms of outreach programmes to schools, as well as informal since people learn from the experience of their visits. Entertainment is seen as a way of competing with other calls on the attention of the visiting public, as well as sugaring the pill of institutional messaging. However, Timothy does not explicitly speak to the role of interpretation in the development process of heritage tourism projects in order to achieve the outcomes of education and entertainment.

The building of meaning in a relatively sophisticated audience is a complex process which involves aspects such as communication theory, passive/active audience transmission models, constructivism and semiotics, consumer theory, ideas of selective reading and cultural capital (Mason, 2005). Copeland (2006) provides a theoretical framework to explain the way that meaning is constructed on archaeological sites and suggests strategies for interpretation: presenting the site with an emphasis on big concepts (such as justice); relying heavily on evidence; treating visitors as thinkers with emerging ideas about the past; mediating the historic environment; valuing exploration; encouraging discourse; assessing and evaluating to improve interpretation.

Moscardo (1996) proposes that interpretation can promote a sense of "mindfulness" in visitors that can have a significant effect on the attitude

Figure 4.1 The HKWP not only raises awareness of the need for wetland conservation, but also provides a welcome relief from the dense urbanisation for the residents of Tin Shui Wai
Source: Photograph by Chunyip Wong, Getty Images.

to conservation on the site itself. As an example of this, Cheung (2008) points to the success of the range of interpretive devices and presentations in attracting, particularly domestic, tourists to the Hong Kong Wetland Park (HKWP), in order to promote both ecotourism and raise awareness of the need for wetland conservation. Having been the Interpretive Planner on the HKWP, I can state with some certainty that interpretation was involved at every point of the project from inception to installation.

Effective management

Timothy (2011) further states that "interpretation is one of the most vital elements of sustainable management at heritage properties .... Effectual interpretive planning is essential." It stands to reason, therefore, that interpretive planning must have a strategically important role in the development of such projects. McIntosh (1999) places the visitor experience at the heart of the heritage management process. Millar (1989) ranks the importance of interpretive planning to management even more strongly when she says that heritage interpretation is the key to a successful management policy for heritage sites and is central to the management process. As well as teaching us about our past, it should act as a starting point that enables the designation of management priorities, underpinning management, marketing and financial decisions and strategies.

Creating a sense of place

Creating a sense of place and place identity is another important role ascribed to interpretation by Uzzell (1996). Indeed, place itself can be seen to be a key theoretical dimension by which to evaluate interpretation as it "captures, in a holistic way, the inter-relationships, complexities and variabilities between visitors, their experience and the site that is being interpreted" (Stewart & Kirby, 1998). The fulfilment of tourism experiences of heritage buildings is considered to have three main themes: visual appeal, personal reflections and engaging experiences (Willson & McIntosh, 2007). Interpretation is intrinsic to all of them. Hems and Blockley (2006) present a series of perspectives on heritage interpretation in the British context and how we can meet the challenge of ascribing value to a place, how we choose which stories to tell and how this impacts on the significance of the place whose stories we relate. They value the visitor as part of the interpretive process to bring "real life into buildings from the past" rather than being guided by the old adage of "bringing the past to life".

Nation building and conflict resolution

In Asian and Middle Eastern contexts, interpretation is meeting the need to create and reinforce nation-building narratives. For example, telling the story of Singapore's wartime occupation under the Japanese through conservation and interpretation is seen to have a social, economic and political value (Henderson, 2007). Teo and Chang (2009) point out how the revitalisation of buildings from the colonial period in Singapore caught new waves of hybridity, eclecticism and nostalgia in the region. Local communities, such as that in Toraja, South Sulawesi Indonesia, can see the benefit of interpretation to "convey local wisdom to enhance the visitor experience" (Kauser & Gunawan, 2017). Pareticularly in the context of contested histories, heritage "can be a safe and neutral ground for mediating political contentions and conflicts" (Park, 2011). In the conversion of the Central Police Station, Magistrates' Court and Victoria Prison in Hong Kong, on which I was the Interpretive Planner, a careful line had to be trod in the storytelling between historical significance, nostalgia, British colonial methods of policing and punishment and such issues as the Japanese Occupation during the Second World War. Opened to the public in 2018, it was an important step in helping to redefine Hong Kong's post-colonial identity.

Why does interpretation get "lost" in some projects?

There has been something of a theoretical and practical void in terms of how the twin forces of interpretation and commodification actually work in relation to heritage tourism products. This interpretation/commodification nexus sees the cultural/heritage interpretive practitioner frequently operating within the context of an architecturally and commercially led project. Within a development team of competing agendas such as new-build architecture or commercial real estate (the practitioners of which have ready tools for quantifying the value of their work to the project), interpretation can sometimes find itself "put on the back burner" as more quantifiable elements of the project take priority. This may be the case even when telling the story of the site is widely promoted as the *raison d'être* for spending large amounts of public money. As more adaptive re-use projects, which involve both public money and the alteration of public heritage assets, come on stream around the world this will be an increasingly important issue if storytelling is to remain at the heart of such projects.

  An analysis of why the interpretation of historical content or storytelling gets lost in these projects was conducted in Hong Kong in relation to the growing trend in heritage revitalisation projects there (White, 2019). This focused primarily on the role of the Hong Kong government in commissioning and managing such projects. Some cynicism was expressed by respondents as to whether the stated intention of such projects was genuinely held by their commissioners. This feeling was compounded by a sense that the impetus to start looking at the interpretive aspect of these projects has come largely from the public and the government has been reactive rather than proactive in this regard.

However, the lack of experience in government in dealing with such complex and sensitive projects was seen as a problem at a fundamental level. Once a project is initiated, it was also felt that there seems to be a lack of engagement with the subject matter in question by civil service project managers and, by extension, a perceived or assumed lack of interest amongst the Hong Kong public. This was deemed to be particularly true at the middle management level of government project administration (one interviewee put it as strongly as, "They're just not bloody interested!"). This had translated into a greater degree of focus on the hardware of conservation projects rather than the software; an emphasis on the tangible over the intangible, building over story.

A possible explanation for this perceived lack of interest in Hong Kong's story was the way local history was taught in the education curriculum under British colonial rule. To some extent, this explains much of the apparent apathy amongst even civil servants running heritage-related projects and the emergence of a new interest amongst the younger generation. It is only with the post-80s generation that Hong Kong people are really beginning to have a sense of permanent identity and nostalgia about the history of their own city. But this also means that without a firm foundation of agreed history, the reawakening of interest can spur a range of contesting versions. Consequently, far from seeing interpretation as a way of ensuring that the narrative element of a revitalisation project is dealt with to a high standard, there has been a tendency to view the process of storytelling within projects with a certain amount of suspicion.

This perceived inherent threat within the contested story of Hong Kong makes the interpretation of it fraught with difficulties and full of pitfalls. This lack of engagement with the content and nervousness about how to deal with it may well be due to the early stage of development of revitalisation heritage projects and developing expertise within the field of interpretation in Hong Kong. These factors have fed into the way that projects have been structured, tendered and managed by governments to date, often leading to unsatisfactory outcomes, until perhaps the Tai Kwun Centre for Heritage and Arts opened in 2016 (see Case study 4).

One can imagine that such issues may dog projects in many developing heritage markets, especially those dealing with contested histories or post-colonial narratives. If the original objective of a project to tell the story of a site is to be fulfilled and not subsumed by or subordinated by other priorities, commercial ones in particular, then a constant emphasis on interpretation and content must be maintained throughout the creative and production process. This means having a sufficiently senior and vocal champion of the story within both the client and consultant team to continually check that the needs of the interpretation are being met and not diluted or overshadowed by other more hard-edged or supposedly immediate considerations.

The process of interpretation in the development of heritage attractions

Interpretation in developing heritage assets represents a significant part of the message communication mechanism, whether that be through human guides or the full array of display techniques available to museums (from static graphics to immersive audiovisual). It enables the heritage stewards to educate and entertain through the deployment of these various techniques for storytelling: to convey a lasting meaning and sense of importance through creating an emotional connection with authenticity; to raise awareness to help in any conservation effort; to allow the targeting of a substantial visitation audience through schools; to act as a potential source of revenue; and it can even be used as a crowd control tool.

Elements of interpretive planning can and should take place to varying degrees throughout the design and implementation process of museum and heritage tourism projects. All too often the need for an interpretive plan is realised too late in the design process when time and money have already been wasted on attempts to reach a design solution without the proper groundwork having been done. Alternatively, an Interpretive Plan is sometimes created at the beginning of a project to raise funds and never referred to again.

Interpretive planning requires a number of core skills and knowledge sets. It is important to be able to assess, analyse and sift large amounts of information quickly, accurately and with a degree of intellectual rigour. The ability to engage and excite various stakeholders in the project to actively take part in interviews and workshops is key to moving the thinking on the project forward to some form of consensus. All of this must be done with a thorough background knowledge of how different audiences access and react to different types of information and techniques of presentation within an experiential context. This can only come from practical experience of designing successful attractions – understanding how a visit can be informative, inspiring and fun. Understanding what design consultants will need to know (in terms of both content and practical project parameters) in the next phase of the project is instrumental in producing an Interpretive Plan that will be of practical use going forward.

As stated, interpretive planning of some kind should take place throughout the project but, where possible, the planner should insist on a first, distinct stage dedicated to interpretive issues prior to any meaningful design being done. Depending on the size of the project, this interpretive stage might last anything between one and six months and result in a deliverable aptly named Interpretive Plan. This is sometimes accompanied by a Feasibility Study or Practicable Plan that looks at practical issues across the site such as physical access and traffic flow (of both people and vehicles). These two documents might then feed into a wider Masterplan for the project in order to raise capital.

The Interpretive Plan aims to turn the principles of interpretation into a reality for a specific site. It aims to be a clear statement of the aims, context, issues, approaches and methods of implementation for that site. It should act as both a strategic framework for building consensus for project objectives, as well as a plan of action for future consultants. What might an interpretive planner be expected to do as part of the process? In essence, it explores the following questions: Why are you interpreting the site? Who is the interpretation for? What will you interpret? And how will you interpret it? Tasks under the scope of works might include:

- Benchmarking and reviewing the best of similar visitor centres locally, regionally or around the world
- Wide consultation with senior members of the client team and relevant departments through interviews, workshops and presentations
- Running workshops to define and test the values and mission statement of the experience
- Discussing and defining key themes to be expressed through an interpretive framework
- Expressing the spatial interrelationship of these themes
- Reviewing and selecting heritage assets to be interpreted, including artefacts and images
- Arranging remedial conservation and care for objects that require it
- Specifying environmental and display case conservation requirements
- Providing a suggested narrative design treatment for each exhibition area

Each project will be different in terms of the ground that the Interpretive Plan has to cover but let us look at each of these in a general fashion:

Benchmarking similar attractions: for major projects, this is a useful exercise to position your project within a regional, national or global context. It is particularly important if the client has aspirations to be world class. This may involve a carefully planned itinerary to visit a number of comparable museums or visitor attractions to review what works and what does not. A list of desirable facilities and elements (e.g. cafe, shop, classrooms, outdoor spaces, etc.) can also be discussed. In a region where there is a high degree of tourist mobility, it also assists in differentiating the offer of your completed project. It is best carried out at a very early stage in the project, ideally at the planning stage before design begins. There is nothing worse than being halfway through the design and the client announcing a worldwide trip to gather ideas. Other side benefits include an opportunity for the project team to bond and get to know each other better.

Consultation with senior management: whilst it is often the case that a project begins through the initiative of a senior manager or director, frequently the development of the brief for the project is left to middle managers. This means that a consultant may receive the brief several months or even a year after the initial discussion of the project. It is not unusual for this brief to have misinterpreted the ideas of the originator of the project. This makes it essential for the consultant to insist on a one-to-one interview with key stakeholders in the project, the more senior the better. This ensures that you can get a firm grip on the aspirations, aims and objectives of the project right from the horse's mouth. It is also important to arrange either individual or group interviews with a wide range of stakeholders, including those who may have run any previous visitor centres within the company or museum, as well as those who may run the end product in the future. This will help identify practical issues which may have a direct bearing on the design.

Defining project values and the mission statement: in conjunction with the stakeholder interviews, it is often useful to hold workshops with various interested groups to define the values of the project (brand values, if you will) and through these the foundation mission statement. This is a good way to remind the client team that it is not your job to invent their story but to enable them to tell their own story. If the stakeholders of the project do not believe in the values of the project, then what hope has it of succeeding? The identity of the finished product will evolve from these values. Various workshopping techniques can be employed, and different ways of engaging potentially reticent members of the workshop should be used such as games and visual props.

Defining key themes: allied to these interviews and workshop sessions, should be some initial outlining of key themes and topics to be explored by the future museum or heritage attraction. This may involve some wide-ranging, in-depth desk research and discussions with experts in the relevant fields or communities. Getting consensus on the major topics to be explored and the desired key messages to convey to visitors will go a long way to getting the design kicked off in the right direction.

Spatial interrelationships: while on the subject of themes, it is also a good time to discuss notional, conceptual relationships between themes. At this early stage, the temptation to start designing should be avoided. It is important to establish connections between themes in order to inform narrative and visitor flow, suggesting adjacencies and volumes of exhibition spaces, facilities and galleries.

Selecting heritage assets: most museums have extensive collections on which to draw for display items. This may require an extensive review with curators of appropriate artefacts and images to support key narratives and messages. Ideally, of course, objects will be selected carefully in order to each have a point to make. But inevitably there are sometimes star objects, sometimes quite sizable, that need to be given a prominent place in the visitor journey and it is best to know this early in the design process. On the other hand, some corporate clients may have very little in the way of collections, in which case a plan may need to be drawn up as to how to go about initiating acquisitions. It should also be remembered that heritage assets can take the form of oral history, which can sometimes provide the most emotive and meaningful content.

Conservation of heritage assets: depending on the asset selected, there may be a need for some form of repair or conservation (for more on this see the next section on "Conservation and authenticity"). This will be particularly true of objects to be put on display. Display conditions should be defined early in the process so that long lead items such as museum-grade showcases can be ordered in good time and a suitable budget allowance made for such expensive items. Conservation specialists should always be employed to carry out any such work and this should not be an area for budgetary or scheduling compromise. Of course, in some cases, the heritage asset may be the site itself, in which case an extensive survey should be commissioned at the earliest possible opportunity.

Specifying appropriate display cases: one of the most frequently underestimated budgetary items in such projects are display cases. Reputable, established museums appreciate the need to protect their objects while on display and so are used to investing in museum-grade display cases. New, private or corporate museums may have estimated a budget before the interpretive consultant arrives on the job. Invariably, the budget for display cases is underestimated and, in some cases, only allows for retail-style vitrines. An early appraisal of the need for environmentally controlled showcases is necessary in order to begin the inevitable fight for an appropriate level of investment for proper conservation display cases.

Suggested design treatments: whilst we are not at the point of designing, it is useful to glean a sense from stakeholders of what kind of experience they foresee for each thematic area. Firm promises should not be made at this stage and everyone should be asked to remain open minded, but it is useful to get the client team to start to think in terms of differentiated experiences for the visitor journey.

Conservation and authenticity

When one thinks of authenticity in a museum context the first things that spring to mind are objects. As we have seen, the careful selection of heritage assets for display and/or conservation is an important part of creating both the storyline and credibility of the visitor experience during the interpretive planning stage. Not only does the authenticity of an object or place contribute to the visitors' experience, it also contributes to the sense that the museum is fulfilling its traditional primary mission of preserving tangible heritage.

As we have seen in Chapter 3, ideas of authenticity can be constructed or manipulated to create a kind of hybrid sense of experiential genuineness, but when looking at individual objects visitors still tend to judge whether they are "real" in various ways. These ways of assessing objects tend to be a combination of perceptions of originality, significance (historical or personal), uniqueness, monetary value, aesthetics and even signs of use or wear and tear. So, any restoration, repair or conservation efforts must be carefully considered in terms of how they will materially affect the object and the perception of its authenticity.

If the museum or heritage attraction is not well established it may not have a conservation department. In this case, it is important that the managers of the institution build a network of specialists (e.g. paper, wood, metal, textile conservators) who can provide condition reports, advice on storage and care and, if necessary, restoration. Discussions around how any conservation works might affect the object can be had between these specialists and other curatorial experts in the field. The wonderful thing about the conservation world is that, for the most part, people are really focused on what is best for the artefact and will freely and enthusiastically enter into these discussions.

What goes for individual objects is magnified when it comes to buildings. At the heart of many heritage-based tourist experiences is some form of built asset. However, conservation considerations of such buildings are rarely simply a matter of returning them to the original state of a single time period. Scratch beneath the surface of many of the world's most famous heritage attractions and the complexity that belies its iconic status is often revealed. The Tower of London, for instance, a must-see of the city's tourist scene, is promoted through images of the Beefeaters, ravens, Traitor's Gate and Crown Jewels. A tourist attraction since the Elizabethan 16th century, it has also been the subject of architectural expansion and rebuild since Norman times meaning that it is a collection of architecture (some overlapping) representing periods from the 11th century, Middle Ages, Tudors, Restoration and 19th and 20th centuries. It presents a coherent brand from a multi-layered, complex reality. Such complex issues require a specialist conservation architect to be part of the team to produce a Conservation Management Plan (CMP) that will guide all aspects of any restoration or revitalisation. This document can also be a useful starting point for interpretive planning as it will map out the key historical, architectural and cultural significances of the property.

Decisions on what to conserve when restoring buildings with such complex layers of history touch on what is regarded as more or less authentic – is it age, condition or architecture that is more representative of a period style? For instance, when fire raged through the state apartments of Windsor Castle, the world's oldest and largest inhabited castle, in November 1992 the subsequent restoration effort offered the opportunity to reinstate the original interior designs commissioned under George IV according to detailed drawings personally signed by the King himself kept in the Royal Collection. According to Sir Hugh Roberts, former Director of the Royal Collection, "The view was that we should try to restore something of the magnificence that George IV was attempting to do but without spending quite the amount of money that he thought was normal." Restoration in this case has arguably created a more authentic look to these rooms as was originally intended, rather than the 1920s interiors commissioned by Queen Mary that perished in the fire.

Another interesting example which gives a sense of the kinds of debate that take place around conservation and the adaptive re-use of heritage buildings is the former Central Police Station in Hong Kong, now revitalised as the Tai Kwun Centre for Heritage and Arts. This compound of heritage buildings was itself the product of a series of expansions since the site was built as a prison in the 1840s, ranging from the mid-

Figure 4.2 A series of exhibits explain the complex evolution of the Tower of
    London's physical form and architecture
Source: Photograph by Chris White.

19th century to the early 20th century with various interior and exterior
additions and styles. Its significance lies in containing some of the oldest
colonial buildings still standing in Hong Kong. However, one of the
oldest buildings on the site decided on 29 May 2016 that it had stood
long enough. I remember well when the Married Inspectors' Quarters

(known as Block 4) partially collapsed that night as I was still working on supervising the implementation of the interpretive design (for more information on this see Case study 4). This historic building was an integral part of the overall site planning and, given that the site was to be one of the foremost heritage revitalisation projects in the region, this presented a real challenge to the team.

Initially, eight proposals were considered: restoration; reconstruction; adaptation; preservation; façade retention; façade and interior retention; total reconstruction; and demolition. These were then assessed based on three criteria: engineering feasibility (whether an option was safe for the building, the site and people); heritage value (whether it would result in insignificant or significant damage to the historic fabric of the building); and contextual value (whether it was compatible with the objective of the revitalisation project). Following this assessment exercise a shortlist of three options emerged: reconstruction (to rebuild the collapsed parts of the building by using modern materials and adaptively re-use it); adaptation (to rebuild the collapsed part in a contemporary design with associated internal alterations throughout for adaptive re-use); and preservation (to conserve the partially collapsed building as found and keep the remaining standing parts of the building for adaptive re-use). There was very much the desire to avoid creating a replica of the collapsed portion that may have been seen as "fake" heritage with a detrimental impact on the heritage fabric of the compound. The final decision on how to recover this partially lost building is subject to further engineering investigations and may involve a hybrid of the shortlisted solutions.

Box 4.1 Case study 4: The Interpretive Plan for the Tai Kwun Centre for Heritage and Arts

Around the time that the revitalised former Marine Police Headquarters was opening (see Chapter 3) in Hong Kong, I was approached by the Hong Kong Jockey Club to get involved with the revitalisation of the Central Police Station (CPS), which also comprised the Central Magistracy and Victoria Prison. This 13,600-square-metre compound contains some of the oldest and best preserved colonial buildings in Hong Kong, dating as far back as the 1850s. As such, the CPS was the largest surviving cluster of heritage buildings in urban Hong Kong; its combination of police station, police quarters, magistracy and prison made it a unique "one-stop-shop" for law and order, and a site of great historical importance.

In 1995, the former Central Police Station, the Central Magistracy and the Victoria Prison were listed as declared monuments. In 2006, the project was taken on by the Hong Kong Jockey Club in partnership with the Hong Kong government and signature architects Herzog & de Meuron were appointed. Two years later, the conservation architect Purcell Miller Tritton (hereafter Purcell) was appointed and produced the Conservation Management Plan (CMP), which laid out a conservation and management model for the site. Purcell's CMP laid out restoration plans tailored for each of the buildings. Work was carried out to the highest of international conservation standards, building by building and room by room, including the successful restoration and reinstatement of 65 per cent of the original timber windows and doors site-wide. Heritage fabric removed as part of the revitalisation work was re-used on the site. Replacements were fabricated as close to the originals as possible.

My company (Winkle-picker Ltd) was appointed Interpretive Planner for the project in 2009. At the time, it was the largest heritage conservation and revitalisation project in the city, and was to set the bar for other revitalisation projects in Hong Kong. A major programme of artefact and oral history collection was initiated to populate these spaces with tangible and intangible objects of interest. Buildings and rooms were appraised for their suitability to be incorporated into the visitor experience and eventually over 1,000 square metres of space was earmarked for interpretive treatment. This usually involved the weighing up of a range of factors such as:

- Historic significance of the building/room itself to the overall narrative of the site
- The conservation status of the building/room
- The degree to which it was adaptable to commercial or museum use
- Its commercial real estate value in terms of location, rentability and likely footfall (those following a heritage trail are more likely to look for out-of-the-way places)
- How well it fitted in to the overall storytelling of the site.

The goals of the Interpretive Plan were outlined as follows:

- The site should be presented holistically with an emphasis on concepts of chronology, change and evidence
- The content providers should be seen as community-wide rather than solely expert-driven

- Visitors should be regarded as active participants rather than passive consumers
- The interpretation should mediate rather than dictate the historic environment for the visitor
- Interpretive strategies should aim to encourage discourse. Visitors should be encouraged to inquire and question
- Assessment and evaluation should seek to discover visitor perspectives and help improve interpretation on an ongoing basis.

The Interpretive Plan laid out a range of provisions to meet the needs of its audience and the diverse nature of the site, including permanent exhibitions (graphics, audiovisual, interactive computer-based, immersive exhibits, etc.), self-guided walks, interpreter-led tours, portable information devices, workshops and demonstrations, special programmes for target groups, lectures and seminars, publications, educational kits, temporary exhibitions, virtual interpretation (e.g. through the website for marketing, virtual visits, post-visit support, etc.), comprehensive outreach programmes (to include the use of a number of the formats above) and interpretation through public and performing arts.

Key locations were identified in all of the major buildings throughout the site, including a prominent location for a high-quality visitor centre to tell the whole story of the site in the Barrack Block, easily accessible from the Parade Ground. The role of each interpretation location was then explained within the context of the overall visitor journey and the history of the site itself, with suggestions for forms of interpretation through the palette of provision listed above.

At the end of a lengthy process lasting nearly ten years, much negotiation and alteration of the Interpretive Plan (which informed the design and implementation of the interpretive elements throughout the project), the renovated Tai Kwun Centre for Heritage and Arts was opened in 2018. It comprises eight major, designated heritage storytelling spaces across the site including a main visitor centre, and major focal rooms in the magistracy and prison featuring the history, stories and lives of people associated with Tai Kwun. It acts as a not-for-profit hub for heritage, arts and culture, with a wide range of multi-purpose and commercial venues not only for Tai Kwun's events, but also for programmes by other organisations and artists-in-residence, aiming to enrich Hong Kong's cultural life through collaborative efforts.

Testament to the strides made in the heritage tourism sector in Hong Kong by this project was that in 2019 Tai Kwun received the

Figure 4.3 The Tai Kwun Centre for Heritage and Arts opened in 2018 as one of the largest heritage revitalisation projects in Hong Kong
Source: Photograph by Chris White.

Award of Excellence in the UNESCO Asia-Pacific Awards for Cultural Heritage Conservation, recognising the project's revitalisation efforts. After four years, the site had attracted over 10 million visitors. In my view, this can firmly be ascribed to placing interpretive planning at the heart of the process.

Conclusion

Storytelling is at the heart of any museum or heritage experience. Interpretation or interpretive planning is the means by which the story is translated into design, with accompanying display and exposition. Key to this process is understanding the intended audience(s) of the experiential product in order to pitch the communication of information at an appropriate level and in an engaging form. As well as telling a story, interpretation should create a sense of understanding, revelation and appreciation, even inspiration. In this way, it can be a call to action for some form of protection or conservation of a natural or built asset. Creating a sense of place or identity is another potential way in which interpretation can contribute to tourism projects. However, even though telling the story of a site is often the *raison d'être* of a project and the deciding factor in the allocation of public funding, it sometimes gets lost, especially in commercially led initiatives. Ways of guarding against this include appreciating the value of interpretation and purposefully embedding it within the structure of the development and management processes for cultural and heritage tourism projects. Allocating sufficient time to commission a comprehensive Interpretive Plan is key to this.

References

Cheung, S. (2008). Wetland tourism in Hong Kong: from birdwatcher to mass ecotourism. In Cochrane, J. (Ed.). *Asian tourism: growth and change*. London: Routledge.

Copeland, T. (2006). Constructing pasts: interpreting the historic environment. In Hems, A. & Blockley, M. (Eds.) *Heritage interpretation*. Abingdon: Routledge.

Hems, A. & Blockley, M. (2006). *Heritage interpretation*. Abingdon; New York: Routledge.

Henderson, J.C. (2007). Uniquely Singapore? A case study in destination branding. *Journal of Vacation Marketing*, 13(3), 261–274.

Kauser, D. & Gunawan, M. (2017). Managing heritage tourism in Toraja: strengthening local values and improving tourists' experiences. *Journal of Heritage Tourism*, 13(6), 1–12.

Mason, R. (2005). Museums, galleries and heritage: sites of meaning-making and communication. In Corsane, G. (Ed.). *Heritage, museums and galleries: an introductory reader*. Abingdon: Routledge.

Mason, R., Robinson, A. & Coffield, E. (2018). *Museum and gallery studies*. Abingdon: Routledge.

McIntosh, A. (1999). Into the tourist's mind: understanding the value of the heritage experience, *Journal of Travel and Tourism Marketing*, 8(1), 41–64.

Millar, S. (1989). Heritage management for heritage tourism. *Tourism Management*, 10(1), 9–14.

Moscardo, G. (1996). Mindful visitors: heritage and tourism. *Annals of Tourism Research*, 23(2), 376–397.

Park, H. (2011). Shared national memory as intangible heritage: re-imagining two Koreas as one nation. *Annals of Tourism Research*: 38(2), 520–539.

Staiff, R. (2014). *Re-imagining heritage interpretation: enchanting the past-future*. London: Routledge.

Stewart, E. & Kirby, V. (1998). Interpretive evaluation: Towards a place approach. *International Journal of Heritage Studies*, 4(1), 30–44.

Teo, P. & Chang, T. (2009). Singapore's postcolonial landscape: boutique hotels as agents. In Winter, T., Teo, P. & Chang, T. *Asia on tour: exploring the rise of Asian tourism*. London, New York: Routledge.

Tilden, F. (1977). *Interpreting our heritage*. Chapel Hill: University of North Carolina Press.

Timothy, D. (2011). *Cultural and heritage tourism*. Bristol; Ontario; New York: Channel View.

Timothy, D. & Boyd, S.W. (2003). *Heritage tourism*. Harlow: Pearson Education.

Uzzell, D. (1996). Creating place identity through heritage interpretation. *International Journal of Heritage Studies*, 1(4), 219–228.

White, C. (2019). *Heritage revitalisation for tourism in Hong Kong*. Abingdon: Routledge.

Willson, G. & McIntosh, A. (2007). Heritage buildings and tourism: an experiential view. *Journal of Heritage Tourism*, 2(2), 75–93.

Further reading

Tilden, F. (1977). *Interpreting our heritage*. Chapel Hill: University of North Carolina Press.

White, C. (2019). *Heritage revitalisation for tourism in Hong Kong*. Abingdon: Routledge.

5 Museum design management

The demand for museum design

It is hard to know which came first – the increasing demand for visitor attractions (sites, museums, visitor centres, etc.) or the increasing number of such attractions that spawned the demand. Certainly, the public money spent on such attractions in many major tourism destination cities has seen a steady increase in the past couple of decades, particularly in European destinations as they vie with neighbours for increased tourist traffic both from within the European Union (EU) and from outside, notably China and the Middle East. And the competition is not just between countries but between towns and cities. Of the relatively little literature written about how heritage attractions come about much of it focuses on their symbolism, semiotics and experience (Boorstin 1964, MacCannell 1976, Leiper 1990) and less on the actual process by which these products are created through the collaboration of governments (local, regional and national) with the creative industries and sometimes charitable donors or commercial sponsors.

Satisfying this demand has often led to a production-led (rather than a consumption-led) approach with the creative industries being seen as vital to underpin the development of a nation's or city's heritage or cultural assets. Often the first port of call for clients are "signature" architects. Architects love to design a museum – the sheer esotericism of it all. Often, in their view, it is the people that mess the clean lines of their museums up, annoyingly intent on what is going on inside of the iconic structure. That is where museum designers come in (if there is any money left after the architects have finished construction of their exterior vision) because to them a museum or heritage environment is nothing without people to experience it. Indeed, what actually matters is how people engage with the museum's content and how they bring their messiness (expectations, prejudices, raincoats, lunches and children) to it.

DOI: 10.4324/9781003369240-8

The opera of design

Museum or visitor attraction design differs from the architectural design process in not so much being the product of an individual visionary or manifesting a single iconic idea. Museum design is multi-disciplinary; if other forms of design (graphic, structural, sculptural, audiovisual, etc.) could be compared to different types of music and dramatic performance, then museum design brings them all together. It is the opera of design. To illustrate this there follows a list of the type of creatives that I have worked with over 30 years in the museum design industry:

- Architects
- Landscape architects
- Interpretive planners
- Museum designers
- Theme park and ride designers
- Graphic designers
- Brand specialists
- Audiovisual designers
- Illustrators
- Film makers
- Scriptwriters
- Composers
- Photographers
- Sculptors
- Diorama designers
- Modelmakers
- Researchers
- Curators
- Artists (including digital installation artists)
- Taxidermists
- Live performers

All or some of these disciplines will be involved in every museum design project. Yet so little that is substantive has been written on the subject of how this process of coordinating such a diverse team of creatives affects the outcome of the product that, for instance, I have yet to find an academic paper which tackles what many professionals in the field might regard as a fundamental decision in the process: whether to appoint an architect to produce a Masterplan for the attraction or a specialist museum designer. It would be my contention that this process,

Figure 5.1 An exhibit on the Arctic tundra at the Hong Kong Wetland Park. Museums and visitor centres can employ a wide range of trades and specialists from taxidermists to modelmakers, all of which need coordinating with the other exhibition techniques
Source: Photograph by Chris White.

and the concerns and interactions between these players and stakeholders, have a major impact on the final heritage tourism product.

Design/supervision or design/build?

A fundamental decision for the client is whether to run the project as a design/supervision or design/build contract. The former will mean that the specialist museum design company designs up to tender stage and then sits alongside the client to supervise the fabrication and installation by the main contractor and its subcontractors. A design/build contract means that the designers need to team up with a main contractor or a main contractor with a design arm within it will be used. There are pros and cons to both approaches. Design/supervision means that the client has specialist expertise to draw on during the production and installation phase which has a vested interest in safeguarding the integrity of the original design vision. However, it does mean a longer tender period, thus extending the overall project programme. A design/build contract may sometimes seem like a more streamlined contractual arrangement for the client, but it does take away the checks and balances between the design and contractor, meaning that it is easier for the latter to cut corners and compromise the design vision. We would almost always recommend a design/supervision contract and it is this type of contractual process that we will look at in more detail.

Royal Institute of British Architects stages

Whatever the type of museum, their design can be carried out by a process that has evolved over the past 30 years (since my first involvement in the industry) and almost certainly decades before that. Then, informal processes were handed down from one generation of professionals to the next with wide variations between companies and markets. When I first began working in the museum design sector, it was just becoming standard to align exhibition design with the Royal Institute of British Architects (RIBA) stages. This introduced more structure and elevated the status of exhibition design within the eyes of clients and (sometimes but not always) architects and other creatives.

In the early 1990s, the RIBA work stages were already 30 years old, but the museum design industry was just catching up with them. Begun in 1963 to provide a framework for architects to use on projects with their clients and bring greater clarity to the different stages of a project, the RIBA system of work has evolved over the years to reflect changing trends in project approaches. Given that, especially with new museums, specialist interior design often works in parallel with architectural design, it made perfect sense to align the processes of the two disciplines. At that time, and further defined in the Outline Plan of Work of 2007, the stages ran from A (Appraisal) to L (Post Practical Completion). The RIBA Plan of Work 2013 reorganised the process of briefing, designing, constructing, maintaining, operating and using building projects into a number of key stages. The core design stages remained fundamentally intact, but were supplemented by a Stage 0 (Strategic Definition), acknowledging the need for greater strategic consideration at the start of a project, and Stage 7 (In Use, see Figure 5.2), to reflect the use and life span of a building. Seven years later this work plan was revised again.

RIBA Stage	0	1	2	3	4	5	6	7
	Strategic Definition	Preparation & Briefing	Concept Design	Spatial Coordination	Technical Design	Manufacturing & Construction	Handover	Use
RIBA stage outcome	Client requirements	Project brief	Architectural Concept	Spatially Coordinated Architecture	Architectural Technical Information	Manufacturing, Construction & Commissioning Complete	Building handed over	Building in operation
Equivalent museum design stage	Feasibility Study (may include an Interpretive Plan) to help the client prepare a brief	Masterplanning (may also include Feasibility Study and/or an interpretive Plan if not already done in Stage 0)	1 Concept Design	2 Detail Design	3 Technical or Tender Drawings	4 Supervision (if not a Design & Build contract)	5 Completion & Handover	6 Defects Period

Figure 5.2 Updated allocation of museum design stages aligned with RIBA Plan of Work 2020

The biggest addition to the new Plan of Work 2020 was a new sustainably aware project strategy, which challenges teams to design with a focus on sustainable outcomes from the outset of the project.

Museum design stages still often vary from project to project and region to region. Usually, they involve some sort of masterplanning and/or interpretive planning (see Chapter 4) followed by design stages often numbered from 1 (Concept Design) to 5 (Completion). Let us look at an example scope of works stage by stage. These may vary, of course, according to the specialist design required for certain visitor attractions, such as a zoo or aquarium. It should be noted that project management companies who specialise in museum projects may also use an adapted version of the Prince2 methodology or their own adapted approach developed over time.

Masterplanning

The Masterplanning phase is a foundational stage of any project that should not be skipped as it can help avoid nasty surprises later on and would normally include a Feasibility Study (or Practicable Plan) and an Interpretive Plan. It might also include Business, Institutional or Operational Plans. The Feasibility Study will look at the practical parameters within which the visitor experience will take place and be operated, including:

- Setting project objectives
- Defining visitor requirements

- Identifying services and facilities
- Reviewing the site and its physical context
- Analysing traffic conditions and connectivity
- Quantitative planning parameters and mode of operation
- Identifying key issues based on the above
- Schedule of accommodation
- Proposed project schedule and next steps

It is often the case that you do not know that you need an Interpretive Plan until a designer asks, "What is this job about?". For a client, that is already too late because the "design fee meter" has started running. The Interpretive Plan may be stand-alone, run in parallel with the Feasibility Study (and other plans) or slightly behind it as certain findings may influence aspects of its direction, which may include:

- Assessment of visitor groups, number and catchment
- Needs and expectations of visitor groups
- Implications of the above for facilities and interpretation
- Site context and statements of significance
- Initial assessment of collections (display, study and reserve)
- Consideration of conservation requirements selected for likely display
- Assessment of need for further accessions (including oral history)
- Potential interpretive themes
- Interpretive strategies and approaches relevant to visitor groups and site
- Implications of the above for operation and management
- Input to schedule of accommodation
- Input to project programme and next steps

Stage 1: Concept Design

Stage 1 (Concept Design) is when the designer takes the client's brief and/or the outcomes of the Masterplanning stage and develops ideas into a concept design. If there has not been a masterplanning phase, it is important that the consultant scrutinises and challenges the client's brief (which may have been put together by people who have never done a project of this nature before) as false assumptions and misapprehensions can be carried forward from this early stage with potentially troublesome consequences for budget and schedule. If not already done, this phase will include an initial analysis of any collections and content research, working with the museum staff to define storylines, individual theme/topic areas and consideration of visitor routes through the space. By the end of the phase there should be an itemised overview of the experience, approximate costings and a detailed project programme. The tasks included in this stage will result in the following deliverables:

- Interpretive Plan (if not already produced in the previous stage)
- Messaging strategy to convey how key messages will be delivered through the exhibition
- Layout plans: bubble plans showing location of themes and content, storyline interactions, adjacency studies and visitor circulation flow diagrams
- Initial Exhibit Data Sheet (EDS) (see Case study 5)
- Lighting, power and data: identifying early any issues related to access and suitability of the environment in relation to the concept ideas being explored
- Conceptual design response identifying exhibit approaches
- A General Arrangement Plan showing key and focal exhibits for each floor (if applicable)
- Concept sketches, mood boards and area visuals
- Graphic styling and hierarchy
- Audiovisual concept ideas with descriptions
- Requirements for the next stage in terms of information from the client or other parties
- Project Programme showing key tasks to be undertaken and identifying any issues affecting the critical path
- Broad Cost Plan of approximate build and production budget (to within an expected accuracy of 20 per cent).

Stage 2: Scheme Design

Once Stage 1 has been signed off (and it is important that this is done as definitively as possible), then there may follow a Stage 2 (Scheme Design) or, depending on how far the Concept Design has gone in defining the experience, the project may move directly into Stage 3 (Detailed Design). Scheme Design is essentially a matter of developing the ideas that have been approved in Stage 1 to a greater degree without entering into technical detail. In this sense, it consists of a development of all the deliverables in Stage 1 including:

- Developed General Arrangement and Layout Plans
- Scheme design computer-generated imagery visuals and elevations of key areas

- Developed example graphic layouts
- Developed content plan with EDS to explain how exhibits will convey key messages
- Initial lighting, power and data plans
- Scheme materials and finishes boards
- Developed budget estimate (to within an expected accuracy of 15 per cent)

Stage 3: Detailed Design

Within Stage 3 (Detailed Design) the consultant will develop the Concept Design or Scheme Design into more technical design. This will mean refining plans for the exhibition space and creating an itemised list of all exhibit elements, including objects, graphics items and audiovisual. It will detail the audiovisual and information technology (IT) hardware and software requirements, interactive and lighting requirements and identify any Health and Safety implications. This will enable a detailed itemised costing and implementation schedule to be produced. The outcomes of this stage will include:

- Detailed design drawings, sketches and visuals
- Detailed General Arrangement plans
- Detailed requirements for service installations, providing information on weights and sizes of exhibits
- Detailed EDS to describe component parts of exhibits and how they function to deliver key messages
- An itemised graphics schedule including sources of images where required
- Draft graphic text
- Final materials and finishes boards
- Detailed lighting, power and data plans
- Detailed implementation schedule
- Detailed itemised cost plan (to an expected accuracy of approximately 10–15 per cent)

Stage 4: Tender Preparation

Stage 4 is when the designer will produce technical drawings and prepare specifications for all aspects of the exhibition fit out to feed into the tender process so that the fabricator or main contractor can become involved. This is sometimes called the Technical Design or Tender Preparation stage. This will result in:

- Technical drawings for all exhibits and exhibition spaces including sections and elevations where necessary
- Technically detailed EDS and specifications for all requirements including material, mechanical, audiovisual, graphics, etc.
- Fully designed graphics with all components in place including dummy text and images
- Fully itemised list of all images, sources and copyright requirements
- Information packages for use in the tender for the selection of main contractors and sub-contractors
- Identification of where it may be necessary to split off an element of the fabrication and appoint directly through the client rather than through the main contractor (e.g. audiovisual, conservation cases)
- Selection and nomination of specialists and sub-contractors where necessary. Preparation of associated information packages for specialist tenders
- Phased manufacture and installation schedules
- Refined itemised cost plan (to an expected accuracy of approximately 10 per cent)

There then follows a tender period during which time main contractors and fabricators scrutinise the tender packages, send queries and prepare tender returns in response to the information they have received. Sometimes this is split out into a separate stage called Tender alternatively it is included in Stage 5 (Construction). Either way, consultants will be expected to assist the client in answering tenderers' questions, analyse tender returns and shortlist potential awardees. There will usually be interviews of tenderers attended by the consultant to help the client to decide which company should be awarded the fabrication contract.

Stage 5: Construction/Production/Installation

Once the contractor has been appointed, the main phase of procurement, on-site and off-site fabrication and installation begin. This may require visits to the contractor's and sub-contractors' places of fabrication by the designer, sometimes in the presence of the client, to sign off stages of productions, mock-ups and prototypes. To this end, a travel budget should be allowed for if fabrication is based overseas. Throughout, the consultant will be responsible for quality control and ensuring the delivery of their own design vision. They will also supervise installation on-site, monitoring defects and ensuring that contractors rectify them. Tasks that the designer will need to perform during this stage include:

- Review and approve construction (or shop) drawings prepared by contractors and suppliers
- Review samples and prototypes
- Review off-site manufacture
- Review on-site fabrication and installation
- Enable and oversee project management meetings (if a project manager is not employed by the client) between the client and contractor, including ensuring effective minuting and actions follow up
- Commission and test the installations and recommend issuing or withholding of relevant certificates
- Assist the client in agreeing valuations and interim payments
- Work with the client to decide whether the Certificate of Practical Completion can be issued
- Assist in preparation of defects list and rectification schedule

Stage 6: Completion and handover

The final stage (Completion and handover) concludes the project and will include final inspections and defects correction, any management training, preparation of technical manuals and any warranties, passing over of as-built drawings and handover of the site. It will also see the closing of the accounts where any issues around variation orders or monies owed are resolved.

Box 5.1 Case study 5: The use of the EDS at Kuwait's Abdullah Al Salem Culture Centre

Provided by: Chris Cawte, Design PM

The fundamental building block of any museum or exhibition is the "exhibit". A sequence of exhibits delivers the curated storyline that communicates the client's desired message. Each exhibit contributes an essential part of the story, ensuring a coherent whole. A single exhibit could be as simple as a piece of audio or a graphic panel. Or, it might incorporate a coordinated assemblage of audiovisual hardware, bespoke software, film, lighting, graphics, scenic and audio work as well as physical elements, as was the case with the reconstruction of the International Space Station created for the Space Museum in Kuwait's Sheikh Abdullah Al Salem Culture Centre (SAASCC).

If the project team can control all aspects of exhibit development and delivery throughout the project, then the outcome will meet the brief and the client's aspirations. Accordingly, we focus on capturing the aspirations of each exhibit – defining what each exhibit will do, how it will look and the way it will function. In the final phase, the focus moves to ensuring that all aspects of each exhibit's "performance" is delivered to a high standard, in a timely manner and within the client's budget.

To define these requirements and manage development and delivery we need a tool that spans from inception through to the appointment of a contractor: a tool to ensure the client's expectations are faithfully passed through to the requirements of the contract specification; a document that can be the official description of each exhibit, record changes in its design and development and provide a focal point for the client and the design team. Most importantly, this document is *the* place where each specialist inputs their expertise and all contributions are coordinated. For instance, does the media description align with the audiovisual hardware? Or, will the setworks accommodate the technical needs of the showcase that integrates with it? This tool is a document we refer to as the Exhibit Data Sheet or Exhibit Description Sheet, the EDS, and it has always been at the heart of how we manage projects. The EDS connects the client's high-level project aspirations and the detailed technical documentation that is used to procure and deliver the works.

For the SAASCC project, four new museums were created to support the Kuwaiti school curriculum, a requirement that was clearly set out in the project brief. In any project, the overall brief sets out the vision for the finished project and defines the client's aspirations. Sometimes, a brief goes as far as to include an overall narrative for the finished experience. However much – or little – information the brief provides, it is the springboard for the creative team to develop a storyline, in a process similar to the way an author sketches out the chapters of a book. In the case of an exhibition, these chapters are most likely to be represented by galleries, or zones, tackling specific aspects of the exhibition narrative. Within the galleries the narrative will be broken down further and expressed through an inter-related group of exhibits, each contributing a key component of the story.

A signed-off synopsis of the narrative of each gallery leads to a first definition of the exhibits that will express these narratives. At this point, we capture an initial draft EDS for each exhibit and issue these to the client and creative team as a focus for their continued development. For SAASCC, the client was then able to check that the exhibits really did reflect the school curriculum, while the creative team had a strong foundation for developing engaging ways to communicate the content.

At this stage, the EDS represents a developing design brief for each exhibit. It includes an Exhibit Code for tracking, and a Working Title for ease of identification. A Brief Description of the exhibit is supported by a statement of the Key Messages that the exhibit is intended to convey and the Exhibit Objectives and intended (Exhibit) Outcomes. If the exhibit is interactive, or "non-static", the EDS provides an outline of the Exhibit Scenario. The EDS almost always provides a place to record the Background Content to be incorporated (perhaps a physical artefact) and any further Content Research needed.

All these sub-headings are critical to how each exhibit contributes to the overall narrative. More importantly, we now have a statement for each exhibit that links back through each gallery narrative to the project brief. This provides the context for the design development of each exhibit and anchors it in a framework that relates to the client's vision and aspirations for their project.

During design development, we expand the EDS so that the initial exhibit brief is complemented by a written description of the design response. The EDS now includes a Construction section which outlines the exhibit's Physical Characteristics and, where appropriate, extends this to descriptions of any Structural Elements, critical Setting Out Considerations, Contractor Design Elements and Infrastructure Needs. This is where, in SAASCC, every aspect of the Space Station exhibit was brought together to ensure a functional exhibit and a seamless experience for visitors.

EDS documents for more complex exhibits also include sections for Audiovisual Hardware, Media, Film, Graphic Design and Lighting, and potentially Operations and Maintenance Considerations and specific Exhibit Risks, which combine to provide a written definition that is as comprehensive as is possible of the intention of each exhibit. We ensure that each specialist consultant is responsible for providing the EDS entries for their specialisms, resulting in a consistent statement of each specialism across the project. If changes occur, they are captured in the EDS, and revised versions are circulated to all parties. Throughout the design development the designers' drawings are seen as supporting the EDS rather than the supporting the drawings.

Approval of the technical development of the design results in a complete description of all aspects of every exhibit. Descriptions include detailed written specifications of all the specialist packages that need to be procured to deliver the finished product. It therefore becomes a relatively simple exercise to turn the information already honed in the EDS documents into a full project specification and supporting text for Bills of Quantities that list the material to be procured for the exhibition.

Taking this forward into the procurement and appointment of specialist contractors we can control the quality of the outputs via a written specification and supporting drawings. Thanks to the EDS, we can trace the development of the specification back to the project brief, ensuring that the finished museum represents the very essence of the client's original vision.

The project team

The team that is required to put together a museum exhibition obviously varies in accordance with the scale of the project but must have at its core the key disciplines of content specialists, designers and project managers. The client should form a working group with representatives from the departments that will be involved in contributing to and eventually operating the museum, with a project champion within the organisation who is able to make decisions and stand by them at its head. Too often the exhibition design process can become stuck through lack of access to senior, decision-making management or sent around in circles by decisions being made by client representatives without sufficient authority to do so, only to be overturned by a more senior manager in the absence of the designers.

The Client Working Group (see Figure 5.3) should include a representative or representatives of key stakeholders in the project which may include:

Archives/Collections: if artefacts or documents (original or reproduction) are important to the project then it is important for a member of the archives or collections team to be part of the working group in order to advise on the provenance, availability and conservation requirements of any object that may be deemed desirable to put on display.
Curatorial/Research: the curatorship of objects into a meaningful narrative and the research necessary to flesh out the outline of a story should ideally come from within the client team (albeit workshopped and

scrutinised by the consultant's interpretive planner), although it is sometimes wholly handed over to the interpretive specialists within the consultancy team.

Education: the way that the education department intend to run the outreach and guiding programmes on the site should be considered at an early stage as it may influence the way the experience is designed. For instance, a fully guided experience will have less need for interactive exhibits than a self-guided one. Space may need to be allocated for permanent education officers to work or guides/docents to rest.

Facilities Management: the people who will be involved in managing, cleaning and maintaining the facility need to be involved from the beginning of the process in order to inform the design team of any useful grassroots issues, as well as suggesting desirable improvements on existing facilities or ways of doing things.

Marketing: as the people who are dealing with how the institution portrays itself to the outside world, the marketing department should be involved to ensure that brand values are represented by the new exhibition or museum, especially if there is going to be any separate branding of the museum or exhibition itself. It can also be useful to have them involved as the project nears completion to discuss timings of launch and associated marketing events.

Property: those responsible for the alteration, management and operation of the building itself should be involved from the earliest moment to ensure that practical real estate considerations are taken into account.

Project Champion: the pivotal person on the client working team should be of a disposition to be decisive and senior (or brave) enough to be able to argue the case to those of equal rank and above on behalf of the project team.

The following disciplines could be represented on the consultant design team (see Figure 5.3):

Project Manager: this person provides a single point of contact for the client team to ensure that lines of communication are clear and that there is a coordinated response to the client's requests and comments. They are responsible for scheduling and budgeting (possibly with the assistance of a quantity surveyor or specialist quantity surveyor on larger projects). Often, the client directly appoints a project manager to represent them, in which case the consultant should have their own PM or account handler to coordinate with them.

Audiovisual Designer and Lighting Designer: these are disciplines that often sit outside the main design consultancy team as sub-consultants. It should be clarified with the client from the beginning whether they expect these elements to be covered under the main design team as they can account for considerable fees. There is also a notorious grey area in terms of story-boarding for audiovisual programs that is usually part of the production stage under a nominated sub-contractor to the main contractor. It should be clarified with the client at appointment whether the design consultant has allowed fees for these elements of work.

Interpretive Planner: a specialist who acts as a go-between between the client content/archives experts and the design team. They will work to devise a messaging strategy, come up with exhibit ideas and possibly write the exhibition text with the client's input. For more information on this role, please see Chapter 4.

Lead 3D Designer: this person should be the promoter of the design vision for the project (possibly with the input of the consultancy's Creative Director) and may be responsible for managing a team of less senior designers to produce the design drawings and visuals throughout the design process. They should be an excellent communicator and inspirational presenter in order to promote the design in the best way possible. They should also be closely involved with the project manager in supervising the contractor during the manufacturing and implementation stage.

Graphic Designer: a traditional museum exhibition will rely heavily on graphic panels to convey information but even experiences with extensive audiovisual may have an important graphical element. This requires an experienced and highly organised individual to lead the graphics team in what can be the most labour-intensive part of any project of this type. Particular attention should be paid to minimising multiple rounds of changes that can be time-consuming and ultimately costly. For instance, while client team members may not feel able to comment on design when it comes to the text they may feel tempted to produce many edits that can have knock-on effects for the graphics team.

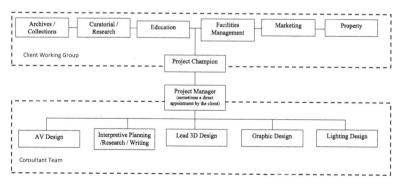

Figure 5.3 Organogram of example disciplines required for the design and supervision process

Building community engagement into the design management process

Why do it?

Even though it seems like an obvious question, why should we engage with communities on museum and heritage projects? Museums reflect the societies in which they are sited. The desire to avoid community engagement is the dirty secret of the museum design world. Imagine a large museum project; the design is ticking along nicely. The design team feels like they know what they are doing, the end of a major stage is in sight and the client seems to have full confidence in what is being done. Someone on the client team then utters the fateful words: "Should we test the design with the public?" The hearts of the design team sink. The idea of unleashing their sophisticated and achingly beautiful design drawings to the great unwashed, the aesthetically challenged, the notoriously fickle and unpredictable people for whom the design is actually intended on fills them with dread. If they were honest with the client, they would admit that they are horrified by the idea. But, what can they say? The design director swallows hard, smiles and says, "Of course!" And sometimes the clients are no better, paying mere lip service to the idea of engagement, deliberately rigging the public consultation to ensure that their predetermined solution is the inevitable outcome of the process.

Those societies which are less hierarchical (so less likely to elevate the status of curator to infallible expert) and with a tendency towards the democratisation of information and valuing experience as well as expertise are more inclined to include a wider range of "voices" in their museums and on their heritage sites. A major reason for greater community engagement is, therefore, to get it *right* (apart from, of course, being the right thing to do).

The primary aspect of the museum design process that community engagement tends to impact in this respect is the interpretation. This can take the form of verifying the provenance of content (including images and artefacts) and confirming information about storylines. Institutions in North America, Canada and Australasia have made great strides in addressing traditional injustices done to aboriginal and native peoples and incorporating them into museum structures and processes.

A second important function of community engagement is enrichment. We all remember how boring museums can be when they solely focus on the material culture of a particular topic; human stories are what bring museum exhibitions alive. Allied to this is the variety of perspectives that community engagement can bring, allowing multi-layered interpretation that can also encompass opposing viewpoints on controversial subjects.

In this sense, the museum, site or exhibition becomes a platform for a range of (perhaps even competing) voices. All sites have value to their communities and this value should be recognised by giving them a say in their development, especially if that site has any connotations of spiritual or cultural community identity.

Finally, all visitor attractions are hungry for new audiences. A selfish reason for incorporating community engagement into institutional arrangements, therefore, is the opportunity that it gives to build new audiences in sectors of the community that might not ordinarily see themselves as museum visitors. Special circumstances may force institutions to focus on particular audiences. The COVID-19 pandemic, for instance, resulted in the collapse of international and regional tourism (see Chapter 6). This meant local audiences became more important to institutions than ever before and finding ways of forging bonds through more consistent engagement, rather than one-off initiatives, was essential. In times of worry and suspicion about public visitation, museums and heritage organisations can be trusted institutions that are a safe space to meet up for enriching and enjoyable social experiences. In light of this sort of situation, it may be possible to find one or two new local audiences that can be persuaded to start visiting in substantial numbers, as well as incentivising clusters of different local audiences of varying sizes to visit. This may involve using all the assets of a venue to attract visitors, even if this is outside of the themes and objects in their collections, such as outdoor spaces (especially useful in pandemics with airborne vectors), food and drink festivals, gardening workshops, family activities or special exercise sessions. Cafés and shops are assets that can be promoted to maximum effect.

Who are you consulting?

One major reason for the aversion to community consultation is that good design often relies on a singular vision. Far from representing a coherent perspective, a community defined from the outside by governments or institutions can themselves be diverse, fragmented or even in conflict. The process of community engagement risks subjecting the design to the destructive or factionalised forces present within the communities themselves. This is a legitimate concern for the design team. However, if the end product is to represent some form of relevance or authenticity, then it must face the sometimes ugly truths within the communities themselves. A sense of conflict has an energy that can be harnessed to power exploration and revelation. Community engagement is not always a warm, fuzzy, feelgood experience.

It is important, therefore, to be clear about *who* you are consulting. This broadly breaks down into two main groups – stakeholders and audiences.

The former has traditionally meant "the great and the good", people with a vested interest in the museum or site, influential people in the process or organisation. However, increasingly stakeholders have been seen as anyone with a "stake" in the project, including people and communities who have a special connection with the collections or site or for whom they have a special meaning. Audiences are of course the people you hope to come or wish to attract to the finished project. This requires a clear marketing analysis for the institution and decisions to be made about the priority of attracting the various market segments. It may mean, for instance, a deliberate decision to target teenagers or specific communities and this will have implications for the interpretation and design going forward. It means that the curatorial approach will make the visitor experience geared towards and relevant for that specific audience, whilst attempting not to alienate other audiences. It is important to be aware of what your audience(s) may already know about a particular topic (including any cultural sensitivities around it), what they would be interested to know and how they would like that information conveyed.

Putting community engagement at the heart of the process

A good way to show genuine willingness to heed community input into the museum or heritage site is to incorporate leaders, members or experts from the community in question at the heart of the project development process. However, careful attention should be paid as to how representative these community figures are and to what extent any one faction within the community in question might be over-represented. This allows ongoing comment to be made as the project progresses, also building trust and opening lines of communication which may allow the channelling of material and information into the project that would not otherwise exist. This method "bakes in" community involvement from the start of the project.

Examining the institutional or project structures into which community representatives can be introduced is one way of looking at community engagement. Another is, as Simon (2010) does, looking at the *types* of engagement that visitors can be involved in which apply equally to types of community engagement. In doing so, she refers to the work of the Public Participation in Scientific Research in the US, applies it to cultural institutions and adds a category of her own (hosted):

- *Contributory:* a very controlled process where visitors are simply asked to contribute objects, ideas or stories through such platforms as comment boards or video kiosks and the project team selects and incorporates them into the experience

- *Collaborative:* as the word suggests, here participants contribute as active partners in the development of specific aspects of the project interpretation and design
- *Co-creative:* where community members are integrated into the project team from the beginning to set missions, goals and creation
- *Hosted:* in this scenario, the institution simply acts as a venue and facilitator (through materials and perhaps funding) to projects wholly originated by the community group.

I would add a category at the lower end of the scale in terms of collaboration (above contributory) and call it "Consultative" whereby an individual or group is consulted at key points in the process, but very much on an informal basis.

Two ways in which community engagement can make a tangible impact on exhibit design are through content and interactive development. In terms of the latter, the rule of thumb is: prototype, prototype, prototype. This is not always possible when working with cost-conscious contractors that will bill the client for every unforeseen variation from the original contract, but is easier to do when the fabrication is in-house.

Evaluation of engagement

Evaluation has long been used in museums to determine the effectiveness of exhibitions. Divided into the three inter-related stages of front-end, formative and summative evaluation, this type of community engagement is directly related to the design and production stages of the project. As the name suggests, front-end evaluation tests the mission and objectives of the project itself and aims to ensure that it sets off on the right track. At inception, the appropriateness of the overall idea for the project can be tested with the community. This should be done with an open mind in the knowledge that it might be outright rejected or significantly modified.

Formative evaluation tests the design as it evolves and aims to input real-world reactions into the creative process. Interpretive planning stages provide an excellent opportunity to elicit responses and input to the content and storytelling approach. The concept design stage allows the design to be tested at an early stage with the community to gauge reactions, appropriateness and willingness to visit. More detailed design stages can garner support and help with getting the minutiae of the design correct, especially in terms of historical or cultural accuracy.

Summative evaluation takes place towards the end of or after the implementation phase to assess the effectiveness of the communication of the original mission and messages. Community visits during implementation and production can build a sense of ownership and anticipation of the opening of the visitor attraction. All of these approaches have the benefit of being controllable by the client and design team, but also the disadvantage of being easily manipulated by those same people in order to get the answers they want (that is, "carry on as you are" or with minor tweaks to the project or design). In the case of summative evaluation, it can very much be a case of shutting the stable door after the horse has bolted.

How do you know community engagement is working?

Traditionally, market research and evaluation by the institutions themselves has been the way of measuring whether the messages of exhibitions are being conveyed and how various segments of the visiting public are receiving those messages. Regular surveying of visitors to permanent and temporary exhibitions can build a picture over time of the likes and dislikes across the museum or heritage site's market segments. This may reveal (or confirm) certain phenomena (such as the average age or level of educational attainment of your audience), as well as sectors of the community that we may need to work harder to attract. Accurate and consistent records of audience visitation and opinions will help build a baseline from which to predict the likely reaction to variations on current exhibitions, promotions or new offerings. Careful attention should be paid to the split between local or repeat visitors and regional or foreign tourists, and their differing tastes and needs. Where communities are multicultural or multi-ethnic, it is important to collect data that reflects this diversity and capture an appropriately complex range of responses to the different aspects of display and operation. This would help to address those specific communities with tailormade offers (not forgetting the need to also have a wider appeal to build bridges across communities), so potentially bringing new audiences, perspectives and voices into the institution.

Conclusion

Museums and exhibitions are complex pieces of multidisciplinary design – they are the equivalent of an opera in the world of music. They require a high degree of structured organisation to be successful. The RIBA stages have been adapted over many years for the purposes of museum planning and design – from Feasibility (Stage 0) to Defects (Stage 6). For the project to run smoothly, the client needs to establish a knowledgeable working group with a senior project champion within it who can take decisions and defend them to upper management on behalf of the project to ensure that it continues to move forward. Within the consultant's team, the specialist skills required will vary from project to project, but clarity should be achieved from the outset as to which disciplines are required and which are being provided by the client. Finally, to ensure that the end product is appropriately representative of the communities it serves, consultation with these communities needs to be built into the development process, preferably into the decision-making of the project structure itself.

References

Boorstin, D. (1964). *The image: a guide to pseudo-events in America*. New York: Harper.

Gardner, J. & Heller, C (1960). *Exhibition and display*. London: Batsford.

Leiper, N. (1990). Tourist attractions systems. *Annals of Tourism Research*, 17(3): 367–384.

MacCannell, D. (1976). *The tourist: a new theory of the leisure class*. London: Macmillan.

Simon, N. (2010). *The participatory museum*. Santa Cruz, CA: Museum 2.0.

Further reading

Lord, B. & Piacente, M. (2022). *Manual of museum exhibitions*. London: Rowman & Littlefield Publishers.

6   Museums in an age of pandemics

The COVID-19 pandemic hits the world

On 31 December 2019, the World Health Organisation (WHO) was informed of an unknown pneumonia in Wuhan, China. On 11 February 2020, this was officially named by the WHO as COVID-19 and by March 2022 over 6 million deaths had been attributed to it.

Museums being museums, when the COVID-19 pandemic hit the world the past was mined for information about how previous pandemics had been dealt with in museums. Between 1905 and 1909, for instance, when the tuberculosis (TB) epidemic was at its height in the US, the American Museum of Natural History and the Smithsonian put on two exhibitions about TB. Although standing in line may not have been the most advisable thing to do in an airborne health crisis, the event proved to be one of the first examples of a blockbuster exhibition on a topic of social relevance. In 1991, eight American science museums joined other organisations to form the National AIDS Exhibition Consortium in order to develop exhibitions on the science of AIDS, as well as safe preventive practices and wider stories to encourage compassion for sufferers. Conferences were held to share best museum practice from the last major pandemic, the Severe Acute Respiratory Syndrome (SARS) epidemic of 2003.

So, whilst responding to global pandemics was not new to museums, the scale of the impact of COVID-19 required some special measures.

Impacts of the COVID-19 pandemic on museums

The reduction in what one might term cultural tourism due to Covid restrictions on movement hit the whole tourist economic ecosystem badly in 2020. With some museums relying on international tourists for 70–75 per cent of their visitors, the closing of transnational borders dealt

DOI: 10.4324/9781003369240-9

a heavy blow. A UNESCO report published in May 2021 on how the COVID-19 pandemic impacted the cultural and heritage sectors reminded us of the interconnectedness of the world's tourist economy. It reported that 90 per cent of countries with World Heritage properties had closed or partially closed them, with visitor figures dropping by 66 per cent (UNESCO, 2021). An International Council of Museums (ICOM) report said that by May 2021 nearly one in ten museum staff had been laid off as a result of the crisis (ICOM, 2021). It also reported that the percentage of museums reporting a loss of income greater than half of their annual revenues was 44 per cent, with almost 70 per cent having a loss of more than 50 per cent of their annual visitors rising to more than 90 per cent for one in five museums.

Museums and heritage sites rely in large part for their audiences on school groups and educational visits, so it is only natural that these activities would have been badly hit by the COVID-19 pandemic. These school visits play an important role in instilling in children the pleasure of discovery in museums and their closure curtails these practices for whole year groups. And as important as museums are for children, students are also important for museums, making up a significant proportion of their annual visitorship. The complete interruption of school attendance and the need for lockdown meant no physical attendance at all of educational groups for long periods. This was seen to impact not only the awareness of communities about the heritage assets or content of specific sites or museums, but also the general civic awareness of the importance of preserving cultural heritage in general. When people are facing a crisis and personal loss, priorities change. It should be remembered that the greatest museum density (measured as the number of museums per million inhabitants) is predominantly in Western Europe and the US, and so issues around museums could be viewed as something of a first-world problem. This contrast is all the more glaring when coupled with the digital divide (often more acute is places with a low awareness of the importance of heritage preservation), where collections have not been digitised and online education is almost impossible.

A museum is not simply a place for visitors; it is also a place of work, research, conservation, organisation and communication. Remote working and other measures taken to protect staff affect all of these activities. Museums also support a network of consultants and freelancers who were particularly hard-hit by the reduction in work, being unable to benefit from government furlough schemes for full-time contracted employees.

Other hard to predict impacts have included increased cases of illegal logging and mining, poaching and vandalism at heritage sites due to the reduction in monitoring and a decrease in managed visitation. One of the

Figure 6.1 The COVID-19 pandemic posed particular challenges to the museum sector with its emphasis on dwell times in public places for collective experiences
Source: Photograph by Mihai Surdu on Unsplash.

greatest concerns among furloughed museum staff, according to a 2020 ICOM survey was the maintenance of stable environmental conditions, with more than 18 per cent of respondents reporting that their systems are not adequate to guarantee object conservation.

As with so many crises, so come opportunities. Just like the return of dolphins to the Grand Canal of Venice in May 2021 due to the lack of tourist pollution, disruption of the status quo in sometimes slow-moving institutions caused by COVID-19 and other pandemics may bring forth new, positive ways of doing things. However, UNESCO's study (2021) found that attempts to tackle the loss of revenue through new ways of generating income were still marginal, with almost six out of ten museums stating that they had not experimented with any new sources of revenue. So, beyond the headline numbers, what actions *did* museums take? And what lessons were learned from the event that might inform museum and heritage operations in a potential age of pandemics?

Measures taken to counter the effects of the pandemic

In the lockdown phase of the pandemic, the main challenge for museums was how to continue to fulfil their mission of providing public access to collections without the physical presence of visitors. Given that lock-down meant that everyone had to stay at home in many parts of the world without exception, the pandemic also made it difficult to maintain the security and preservation of collections. As lockdown restrictions eased, and visitors were allowed to start returning to venues in limited ways, the important thing was how to implement distancing and hygiene requirements for them. And as things return to some sort of normality, museums continue to reassure the public of their vigilance and preparedness for any future pandemics.

At the epicentre of the epidemic outbreak, some lessons might be drawn from how the Chinese government and museums dealt with the crisis. Almost all Chinese museums closed a day after the city of Wuhan locked down, at the end of January 2020. In early February, China's Ministry of Culture and Tourism launched online public culture and tourism services, allowing viewers to browse 30 virtual exhibition halls of the National Museum of China and search for information about historical relics at the Palace Museum. Many of the country's provincial museums developed a centralised website to gather their resources such as virtual exhibitions, online storage and online shopping. Chinese museums also collaborated with some online platforms for livestream events, moving thousands of exhibitions online which attracted billions of users. For instance, China's Palace Museum, or the Forbidden City, conducted a two-day live event during which museum staff took viewers on tours of the ancient imperial mansions, cultural relics and the natural environment, attracting over 100 million views. In terms of reopening, museums, memorials and cultural heritage sites in low-risk outbreak regions were allowed to gradually resume operations. In medium-risk regions, heritage sites and museums had to make a clear distinction between open, outside areas which could open to the public and indoor areas which had to remain closed. Visitors had to make online appointments on staggered visiting times, with track and trace mobile app, face mask and social distancing requirements. The Shanghai Museum, for instance, released 2,000 online appointments every day, 30 per cent of its capacity (Zhang, 2020).

Looking around the world, the steps taken by museums to continue their missions and reach their audiences primarily divided into digital and physical measures.

Digital measures

Following the outbreak of COVID-19, many measures were taken for museums to continue their work of providing access to collections and the knowledge associated with them, including a greater emphasis on outreach by virtual means and digital tools. Such things as digitisation programmes, the development of virtual visits and the use of social networks proved their worth at this time, but also highlighted the digital poverty dividing social classes within nations and between global regions. Internet access itself is unevenly distributed around the world and the facility to digitise collections is fraught with potential obstacles for institutions other than the iconic and well-resourced. For instance, the collections themselves need to be in an organised enough state, with a sufficiently up-to-date inventory, which (although one would think this should be the primary role of museums) is not always the case. There needs to be a minimum of IT infrastructure and equipment (such as photo-taking, scanning and computer facilities) with skilled staff to carry out these various operations. The "big" museums such as the Louvre were able to do this and announced headline-grabbing launches of complete online collections, so grabbing an even greater share of online traffic.

However, if the conditions exist for expanding the online offer of locked-down or visitation-restricted institutions, it can be a relatively cost-effective way (and possibly the only one in a pandemic-hit region) of continuing its mission of providing access to collections and raising awareness to issues related to them. Ways and means of doing this included using existing digitised resources, putting events online, increasing social media activity, creating special content around the idea of lockdown itself and professional activities in the context of lockdown. There were even unexpected success stories such as the volunteers of ferries, bargemen and blacksmiths of the Black Country Living Museum in the UK that became TikTok stars with tens of millions of views.

Work that has been done on digitisation of collections by museums, perhaps for 360° tours, virtual museums, online publications or digital exhibitions, can be re-used to give them a new lease of life. Prior to lockdown, many events or exhibitions had already been scheduled and so it was a natural decision to try to host these in some form online, often via social media, either live or recorded, and downloadable or available on digital platforms such as YouTube. Consequently, there was a greater appreciation among museums of the need to develop their social media activities (especially on Facebook, Twitter and Instagram) or launch a YouTube or SoundCloud channel. This helped to partially transform and diversify some of museums' digital offerings.

Empty museum galleries offered unexpected opportunities to create special content around the idea of museums in lockdown, such as tours behind the scenes or from the viewpoint of fictional visitors, as well as participatory community projects examining the experience of lockdown for people who would normally be visitors, the results of which would become part of the museum experience and collection. Many museums encouraged people within the local community to record and submit photos of life under lockdown.

Finally, time freed up not dealing with visitors or site-specific issues allowed museum professionals to organise virtual conferences to explore and discuss the state of the sector, particularly in the face of such pandemics, as well as have time to be more creative in thinking of ways to engage with their audiences. These and other ideas for an expanded social media presence included:

- Encouraging existing followers to advocate for assistance for museums during the crisis
- Proactively looking to engage with digital partners and open online discussions
- Using more live streaming platforms for broadcasting events
- Unique campaigns that spread virally (think the Shedd Aquarium's penguins being filmed roaming the visitor experience)

Whilst outreach through digital tools would at first glance seem like an ideal and innovative extension of a museum's mission, an analysis of the investment in social media of Italy's 100 most frequented museums, showed that although the online activity of these institutions often doubled in comparison with previous activity, it still paled in comparison with the interaction afforded by a physical museum visit (UNESCO, 2021). The development of virtual museums, again much touted as a new way to bring meaningful access to collections, were seen to suffer from a simple attempt to replicate the visitation experience rather than extend the experience by capitalising on the potential of online digital technology.

Physical measures

As official COVID-19 restrictions were lifted in various countries, museums there faced some difficult choices. When would it actually be safe to reopen without risking spread of the disease? How should museums decide between the costs of operating with lower income or staying closed with no income but fewer overheads? And would people come back? Uncertainty as to whether lockdown would be reimposed added to the conundrum.

The first and perhaps most complex issue for all institutions to deal with was the individual circumstances, fears and anxieties of their own staff. These are the people that will need to feel confident and able to reassure the public, so they themselves need to be sure they are fit and mentally prepared for the challenge of returning to work, possibly after a long period of furlough. Staff may have problems with lack of childcare (if schools are still closed), their own or relatives' health issues, or concerns about their own vulnerability or that of family members. Public transport may be disrupted, so making it difficult to get to work. Volunteers, which many museums rely on, who are often older and so at higher risk may decide it is more advisable to stay at home.

The staffing plan that one usually has to run the museum may need to be reorganised significantly to have more people dealing and communicating with the public about new measures. These new measures will need to be explained to staff and they may even need special training for such things as more thorough cleaning rotas. Staff need to understand any new procedures and how to implement them to make sure that visitors have a fulfilling, relatively stress-free experience. To take one small example, who will staff the entrance to ensure people are using their track and trace apps, taking temperatures or administering hand sanitisers? What do you do if a member of public is not complying with any of these procedures or fails the temperature test?

Most museums implemented some form of visitor number limitation and human traffic flow measures, including timed ticketing (even for free-entry venues), visitor number restrictions and one-way systems, and others such as:

- Contactless admission processes including converting all doors (interior and exterior) to hands-free entry
- Using digital payment platforms and refusing all hard-cash payments
- Requiring visitors (and staff) to wear masks with a stock to hand out if a visitor does not have one
- Frequently spaced hand sanitiser stations
- Barring the use of or removing hands-on interactive exhibits
- Replacing printed gallery guides with smartphone audio guides
- Closing the café and shop
- Making cleaning and sanitation a task conducted frequently during opening hours to reassure visitors, and advertised as such

An example of the degree to which visitor numbers were limited is Beijing's Palace Museum which capped its attendance at 5,000 visitors per day, a huge reduction (94 per cent) from its usual 80,000 visitors per day. This cap was subsequently increased to 8,000 visitors per day with QR code pre-booking, mandatory face masks and hand-sanitiser administration.

Figure 6.2 The use of touch screen interactives, such as these at the National Maritime Museum Greenwich, is a major hygiene management issue, requiring in some cases that such exhibits be temporarily out of service

Source: Photograph by Chris White.

Box 6.1 Case study 6: Measures taken by the Old Royal Naval College, Greenwich during the COVID-19 pandemic, 2020–21

Provided by: Helen White, Senior Interpretation Manager, Old Royal Naval College

The Old Royal Naval College (ORNC) is the centrepiece of Maritime Greenwich, a UNESCO World Heritage Site with a long and celebrated 500-year history. Today it is a diverse cultural destination and one of London's most popular venues, filming locations and visitor attractions, attracting over 1.2 million visitors a year. It comprises a spectacular complex of Grade I-listed buildings founded in 1694 and designed by Sir Christopher Wren and Nicholas Hawksmoor to house the Royal Hospital for Seamen. From 1873 to 1998 the site was occupied by the Royal Naval College. Several of the buildings are currently occupied by the University of Greenwich and the Trinity Laban Conservatoire of Music and Dance. Highlights of the visitor experience include the Painted Hall, the Chapel and a Visitor Centre explaining the history of the site and housing temporary exhibitions.

In response to the COVID-19 pandemic, and in line with UK government instructions, the ORNC closed to the public on 17 March 2020. At first it was anticipated that the closure would last about a month, but it soon became clear that this was to be a longer-term situation. The significance of the site as a through-route became apparent and on 8 June the east-west College Way re-opened to allow pedestrians and cyclists to travel across it in the daytime at weekdays to relieve pressure on the adjacent road and pavements: members of the public could not linger to enjoy the site as a visitor. The ORNC opened for visitors again on 13 July 2020, with social distancing, heightened cleaning and mask-wearing measures in place. Events such as the annual September Open House weekend (when normally private spaces are opened up to the public) took place with reduced capacity. From 5 November the visitor-facing parts of the site were again closed as England entered its second national lockdown, re-opening on Wednesday 2 December. As London was placed in 'Tier 3' measures on 16 December 2020, the majority of the ORNC visitor offer was closed yet again and did not re-open until 17 May 2021, when restrictions were lifted.

At the start of the pandemic the organisation needed to develop a range of responses quickly. It was fortunate that it had an "oven-ready" online offer in the pipeline. A major National Lottery Heritage-funded project to conserve and reinterpret the Painted Hall had included a Virtual Tour: work to complete this was now accelerated and it went live on 2 April 2020, just over two weeks after the site itself had been closed to the public and at a time when government measures allowed people to leave their homes only for essential shopping or medical reasons, or for one form of physical activity per day. The Painted Hall Virtual Tour is of extremely high quality and was short-listed for the London *Time Out*'s 'Time In' Awards that were launched in response to the changed circumstances of the pandemic.

As the site gradually re-opened over the summer of 2020 other technology came into play. A series of self-guided tours that can be downloaded to mobile phones was developed: guided tours returned only gradually, with reduced capacity and mask wearing in place. When the indoor parts of the site could be re-opened, many of the items that might be handled by more than one member of the public were absent because of fears about the risk of infection via touch. 'Treasure chests' full of handling items remained padlocked, and sea explorer bags (containing activities for children) and the printed books that visitors can use to navigate the Painted Hall were kept in store: only in the spring of 2022 did the reintroduction of these items begin. The headphone multimedia guides, an essential part of the Painted Hall interpretation for a high percentage of visitors, were reintroduced with a robust system of disinfection between usages in place, and visitors were encouraged to use their own headphones or earpieces where possible.

The lockdowns in November and December 2020 (the latter lasting until May 2021) meant that an exhibition on "Black Greenwich Pensioners", which opened in October 2020, had only a six-week run and was transferred to an online format. The associated lecture series was replaced by a series of podcasts, and a live performance planned for the Painted Hall became a short film, available on the ORNC website. The Covid restrictions in place in the autumn of 2020 and the subsequent closure of the site inevitably meant that valuable opportunities for engagement with local schools and community groups were restricted.

However, from the start of the first lockdown in the spring of 2020 to the beginning of 2021, the ORNC developed a range of online learning resources aimed at schools and families who were home schooling. Videos of the most popular school workshops, activities and "draw-alongs" were made available, free of charge, online. In May 2021, following the easing of restrictions, school groups started to return to site, taking advantage of new "Covid-safe" sessions which ran until the Prime Minister's "Living with Covid" statement in February 2022. During this period, school visits were restricted to one "bubble" (a group of children who were allowed to mix with each other but not with those outside that group) every other day to allow for the quarantining of materials and the cleaning of spaces. All adults were required to wear either face masks or visors and to sanitise their hands regularly.

Figure 6.3 "Widespread grief and hysteria" is a headline that could have been written about the COVID-19 pandemic but was the reported reaction of the British people to the death of Nelson, as depicted in the ORNC's Nelson Room audiovisual experience opened in 2022

Source: Photograph by Chris White.

The Old Royal Naval College was able to re-open in May 2021 with a strong visitor offer. In particular, the return of Luke Jerram's *Gaia* installation made the Painted Hall a destination for new, younger audiences (among them aspirant Instagram stars!). The reduction in tourism encouraged a refreshed focus on attracting local and London audiences, combined with a readiness to respond quickly to the return of tourists as people began to move around again. The return of corporate hospitality and filming provided a welcome fillip to the ongoing sustainability of the site.

Future trends in an age of pandemics

Whilst most of the temporary physical measures are relatively easy to rein-state if the need arises again, are there signs that more permanent changes to the way museums design their spaces are likely? Visitors are now used to planning their visits more carefully, including advanced purchase of timed tickets to avoid crowding lobbies. This is likely to continue with perhaps an even greater reliance on mobile devices to deliver up-to-date information on potential congestion in specific spaces. A greater emphasis on allocating more outside spaces, where infection risks are reduced, for overflow and group gatherings may also become a trend. Social distancing markers that have so far been temporary and, often peeling, tape on the floor may well be incorporated permanently in tiles and carpet wayfinding.

Interactivity has been the buzz word for so long that it is hard to imagine museums without exhibits to touch and touchscreens to interact with, but the hygiene risks and additional cleaning required may force a rethink. People's personal devices being the interface with the museum gallery may become the norm. However, this will be a particular chal-lenge for children's museums which promote themselves on hands-on interactivity and for whom mobile devices are not an option.

More fundamentally, the success of museums has so far been judged by the metric of visitation numbers. This may change, which in turn has implications for capital investment in projects and the way that museum architecture is envisioned. Data-driven analytical tools of how visitors use, flow through and interact with space will become increasingly important in helping shape the creation of these public arenas. Minimising visitor flow pinch points and places where people are in close proximity, such as lifts, will also become second nature for architects and designers. The spacing of exhibits may require greater breathing room (literally) and the flow around them may mean less free flow to ensure that visitors do not mingle so much. Some visitors might feel comfortable with a pre-scribed route, thinking that it would take them past all the masterpieces without having to think too hard, but for regular visitors this may prove frustrating if they just want to see their favourite work of art. Graphic panels on walls requiring visitors to crowd around to read an introduction to a series of exhibits, for instance, may need completely rethinking.

The very justifiable fear is that the economic downturn caused by the pandemic and the inability to stage events will mean a significant drop in sponsorship and donor income for museums, coupled with ongoing visitor restrictions, long into the future. There may be a trend for museums to downsize in terms of operations whilst aiming to maintain their core missions.

Conclusion

The arrival of COVID-19 was a major challenge to the tourist industry and by extension the museum world. It is unlikely to be the last such event in our lifetime, so what lessons have we learned that might be instructive going forward? Remote working is suited to some forms of curatorship activity but it is hard to conduct collection or site conservation and security under such limiting circumstances. The museum's mission to provide public access to collections can be partly fulfilled by an enhanced online presence but often this means that larger, well-funded institutions just grab an even bigger share of the attention. The lifting of physical visitation restrictions requires first that institutions ensure their staff are confident, able and willing to return to work and well-trained in new preventative public health measures. Looking forward, when physical visitation becomes a problem, there need to be new benchmarks for the success of an attraction other than pure visitor numbers. There is still considerable scope for innovating in relation to how museums interact with their audiences in an age of pandemics.

References

Burke V., Jørgensen D. & Jørgensen F. (2020). 'Museums at home: digital initiatives in response to COVID-19', *Norsk Museumstidsskrift*, 6(2): 117–123.

International Council of Museums (ICOM) (2021). *Museums, museum professionals and COVID-19.* Paris: ICOM.

United Nations Educational, Scientific and Cultural Organisation (UNESCO) (2021). *UNESCO report: museums around the world in the face of COVID-19.* Paris: UNESCO.

Zhang, Y. (2020). *What Chinese museums did during their month-long closure,* 10th *July 2020.* American Alliance of Museums. https://www.aam-us.org/2020/07/10/how-chinese-museums-closed-and-reopened-during-covid-19.

Further reading

International Council of Museums (ICOM) (2021). *Museums, museum professionals and COVID-19.* Paris: ICOM.

United Nations Educational, Scientific and Cultural Organisation (UNESCO) (2021). *UNESCO report: museums around the world in the face of COVID-19.* Paris: UNESCO.

Part III

People

Introduction

The design world is full of influential and colourful characters. Museum design as a specialist creative discipline dealing with high-level concepts, architectural spaces and cutting-edge technology could be said to attract more than its fair share. For a long time, such personalities have pioneered museums for tourism without specific recognition commensurate with their contributions. We intend to look at an admittedly select few of these.

The polymathic nature of museum design seems to attract correspondingly wide-ranging intellects. John Ruskin (1819–1900) certainly fitted that bill, with interests spanning art, architecture, nature, tourism and the spiritual well-being of non-elitist audiences. He recognised the value in connecting us with authentic representations of the past, as well as creating aesthetically meaningful spaces within which to engage with museum and touristic experiences.

Another polymath who should be better known in the pantheon of British designers is James Gardner (1907–95). Designer of the QE2 ocean liner, an important creative influence behind the 1951 Festival of Britain and founder of one of the world's most successful early museum design companies, Gardner almost single-handedly established museum design as a burgeoning creative sector in the UK.

With the museum design sector taking off in earnest over the past 40 years, particularly in the UK and the US, the history of commercial museum design companies themselves has become the subject of collection and research at universities such as Leicester (with its long-established Department of Museums Studies) and Brighton (with its Design Archive). The likes of Ralph Applebaum (RAA), Bill Haley (HSD), Steve Simons (Event Communications), Peter Higgins (Land) and Stephen Greenberg (Metaphor), all warrant a chapter in this

DOI: 10.4324/9781003369240-10

section. However, I have chosen to feature Alex McCuaig (MET Studio) as a direct link to James Gardner and someone with whom I worked for over 14 years.

7 John Ruskin

Learning to look

Finding John Ruskin

Like many people, I first came across John Ruskin on a walk. Or rather, I came across a commemorative stele on the edge of a picturesque view of Derwent Water in England's Lake District. On one side it reads:

> The first thing which I remember as an event in life was being taken by my nurse to the brow of Friar's Crag on Derwentwater.

On the other:

> The spirit of God is around you in the air that you breathe, his glory in the light that you see and in the fruitfulness of the earth and the joy of its creatures. He has written for you day by day his revelation as he has granted you day by day your daily bread.

This stele is a memorial erected to John Ruskin shortly after his death in 1900 by fellow conservationist Hardwicke Rawnsley. John Ruskin (1819–1900) is frequently described as a "polymath". What does this mean? As anyone familiar with the Polymath brand of crossword puzzles in the *Financial Times* will be aware that it requires one to be deeply knowledgeable across a wide breadth of intellectual, artistic, social and spiritual disciplines and subjects. He is known for placing the examination of art and architecture at the heart of a moral critique of the predations of the industrial age in Victorian England. For him, some simple stonework of a gothic cathedral could crystallise all that was right with medieval society and all that was wrong with his own epoch, driven as it was by the twin evils (as he saw it) of industrialisation and capitalism.

Born into relative prosperity in Camberwell, South London in 1819, he had Scottish ancestry and was brought up by his mother in the

DOI: 10.4324/9781003369240-11

Evangelical Presbyterian Christian tradition. His background was over-shadowed by the mania experienced by his father's side of the family. Education, travel and collecting were central to his upbringing, forging habits and tastes that were to inform his intellectual life going forward.

His collected works form 39 volumes of essays, diaries and poetry. His first important work was *Modern Painters Volume I* published in 1843 at the age of 24 which targeted the traditional art establishment (who fêted the 17-century picturesque painters of Italy and Holland) and championed contemporary British painters, especially J.M.W. Turner. It also presented a challenge to the rules of art criticism laid down by the likes of Sir Joshua Reynolds decades previously at the Royal Academy. *Modern Painters* was a clear statement of the evangelical eye with which he viewed art as being revelatory of God's works, "the universal system of nature".

The desire for connection

In 1851, Ruskin wrote an essay on "The Nature of Gothic" as art in his great work *The Stones of Venice (Volume II)*. This was to act as a platform on which he based much of his artistic and social commentary and a metaphorical vehicle for what he thought about the ills and remedies of the world around him. In particular, he saw "the fact that every building of the Gothic period differs in some important respect from every other" as a direct rebuke to the mass production of beam, brick and block that had been ushered in by the age of capitalist industrialisation. Ironically, the most celebrated examples of Gothic revivalism called for by Ruskin in architecture, such as London's St Pancras station opened in 1868, were made possible by the very techniques of mass production he abhorred. However, it was in this requirement for perfection that he saw tyranny, an aristocratic aridness, whilst the tell-tale marks of the stone carver's or the carpenter's tools spoke of the raw, vital individuality of the craftsmen themselves. The imperfections of each gothic building were not to be disparaged but celebrated as breathing authentic life into the building:

> Go forth again to gaze upon the old cathedral front, why you have smiled soft and at the fantastic ignorance of the old sculptors: examine once more those ugly to cleanse, and formless monsters, and stern statues, anatomiless and rigid; but do not mock at them, for there are signs of the life and liberty of every workman who struck the stone; a freedom of thought …
>
> (Ruskin, 1851)

He put the alienation of the contemporary working person's experience of labour at the very heart of the cause of a degeneration in the nation's artistic, cultural and ultimately spiritual fibre. Evidence of the thought process of the creator (be they craftsmen or God) seemed to Ruskin the reason for art. His views on art and artisanship are a perpetual yearning for connection with the craftsman, with different experiences, with the past, with something profoundly human and at the same time godly. In this sense, Ruskin was a true polymath, not merely knowing about many different areas of human endeavour and experience but also making connections between them.

The transformative power of tourism

This desire for connection and an emphasis on thought process over outcome can also be seen in Ruskin's influence on heritage and tourism. Travel was something that his family prioritised and, in this sense, Ruskin was privileged. In 1833, while he was still a teenager, he went with his parents across Europe from Calais to Flanders, Mont Blanc, the Black Forest, Lucerne, Como, Milan and Genoa. Whilst he followed the conventional routes of the Grand Tour (visiting Venice with his family in 1835 and touring Italy in 1845) and upland Britain (first visiting the Lake District in 1824), he is credited with bringing new ways of seeing and experiencing tourism to upper-, middle- and, increasingly, working-class tourists in late 19th- and early 20th-century Britain. "What he provided were new ways of seeing and imagining, new contexts and meanings and a new moral vision which transformed the rhetoric of the experience, and, at least for some people, its actual nature" (Hanley & Walton, 2010). Suspicious as he was of anything that smacked of the mass Cook's Tours approach, he championed what one might see as the ideal of cultural tourism as an individually validated experience which results in some kind of enriching learning outcome.

Whilst Thomas Cook undoubtedly made travel more accessible for ordinary people beginning with his first 15-kilometre train trip for more than 500 people in 1841 (Timothy, 2011), the social mobility that might be a by-product of tourism was seen as less important by Ruskin than the transformative power of the cultural experience itself. Far from being a conservative influence attempting to preserve monuments and landscape in aspic, there is something radical about his aesthetic, anti-capitalist approach that communicates an intense sense of urgency; the objects of his gaze should be both accessible and able to be appreciated by audiences from all walks of life. He even ventured into providing practical, pamphlet-sized guides, a form of interpretive aid for walks, that negated the need for transporting the traditional travel tome. For the British working classes at that time, however, the usual form of holiday was a working one and overseas travel for leisure almost out of the question.

Conservation for the nation

The likes of Wordsworth, Byron and Scott were central to an idea of the essential power of nature and landscape in shaping national character. This was particularly the case in terms of holding up an almost mythic northern England and Scotland as a kind of idealised alternative to the smoke-stacked cities and dark satanic mills of industrialised Britain. Their elegiac experiences of the bond between man and his natural landscape speak of a visceral connection in which we are hewn by the same forces that shape the stones from which we build our homes. This led directly to a movement to preserve areas of outstanding natural beauty, a nascent conservation movement born in the fells and lakes of Cumbria.

Wordsworth began writing guide books to the Lake District in the north west of England in the 1810s and summed up a desire for conservation of the area when he wrote that it was "a sort of national property, in which every man has a right and an interest who has an eye to perceive and a heart to enjoy". Another denizen of the Lake District, Canon Hardwicke Rawnsley (later to erect that monument to Ruskin) founded the Lake District Defence League in 1876 and worked with Octavia Hill to create the National Trust for Places of Historic Interest or Natural Beauty in 1895. The resulting National Trust Act of 1907 describes its aims as:

> To promote the permanent preservation, for the benefit of the nation, of lands and tenements (including buildings) of beauty or historical interest; and, as regards land, to preserve (so far practicable) their natural aspect.

There is a sense in these early definitions of heritage, therefore, that it is more than a legacy or inheritance (which can after all be negative in the sense of historical "baggage"), but that it is positively beneficial, that it can be enjoyed and that there is shared ownership of it. This shared sense of heritage is seen as contributing to local, regional and national identities – essential to the 19th-century projects of European and American nation building. However, as pointed out in Chapter 1, whose heritage one is preserving can be contentious as "heritage benefits someone, and usually disadvantages someone else" (Howard, 2003).

The sensual faculty of the eye

Ruskin believed that "the most beautiful things in the world are the most useless" and this could be a clarion call for museums and heritage organisations around the world. He has something of a reputation for being a thundering art critic full of righteous zeal, but what can so often surprise us is the fact that he really cared what we see. He cared that we see the detail in a gothic arch, a cottage, an oak leaf, a bird or a mineral. This can be said as much of the grandest building in Venice as of a humble piece of moss by a riverbank. He desperately wanted us to learn to look not for his sake but for our own enjoyment. He was not talking to us as fellow professionals but as fellow human beings to whom these things should be important as they enrich our lives. He included us in his gaze (his "sensual faculty of the eye") so that we may be elevated not by any sense of false superiority but by active visual participation in the world around us. His inclusivity was something that speaks directly to us, even today. And this mission that we should learn to look at the world differently can be said to be shared by the best museums.

The idea of a visitor experience is profoundly Ruskinesque. He was all about the experience. For instance, Ruskin praised J.M.W. Turner's painting *San Benedetto* not because it faithfully represents a particular place in Venice but rather because it was an evocation of an experience, an impression of how a visitor feels about Venice:

> there being no church nor quarter belonging to that saint on either side of the Giudecca .... The buildings on the right are also, for the most part, imaginary in their details ... and yet, without one single accurate detail, the picture is the likest thing to what it is meant for – the looking out of the Giudecca landwards, at sunset – of all that I have ever seen.
>
> (Cook & Wedderburn, 1904)

He went on to double down on this and say that it was "all in all ... the best Venetian picture of Turner's which he has left to us". Whilst he was passionate about direct experience and authenticity, I feel he would have been understanding of many visitor experience's attempts to provide access to, explain and distil the essence of many heritage sites, particularly for a general, non-connoisseur audience.

Ruskin the collector

Ruskin is known as something of a collector but in fact he earned very little money during his lifetime, and it was largely his father who invested in art on his behalf. The walls of his bedroom in Brantwood in the Lake District were full of Turner watercolours that had been bought for him. Such was his love of these paintings that he had a special travelling box to enable him to take them as a very personal form of travelling exhibition. He donated large collections of art and geological specimens to museums in Oxford and Sheffield. He also collected nearly 1,500 diverse works of art, including drawings by himself and other artists, prints and photographs, for use in the Drawing School he founded at Oxford in 1871. The Drawing School was intended to train ordinary people who "might see greater beauties than they had hitherto seen in nature and in art, and thereby gain more pleasure in life". Ruskin gathered a collection of drawings for his students to copy over 15 years ranging from watercolours by Turner to book illustrations. He divided the collection into four main series: exemplary works of art, practical examples, those for students from outside the University and those for undergraduates. They were a carefully thought-through resource and study collection for a structured art curriculum.

"All the Pre-Raphaelites ..."

Ruskin clearly believed in the potential for good of museums and saw them as repositories of national treasures that could unlock culture for the masses. He put this theory into practice by helping to plan the Oxford Museum of Natural History, opened in 1860. With his interest in architecture, he had a guiding hand in the design and decoration of the museum's building itself, and it now stand as one of the prime examples of the Pre-Raphaelite vision of science and art. Ruskin's joy at being able to get involved with the design of the museum through a friend was evident:

> I can do whatever I like with it ... I shall get all the pre-Raphaelites to design one each an archivolt and some capitals— and we will have all the plants in England and all the Monsters in the museum.

The Pre-Raphaelites were cut out for museum design. They believed that art should show people the truth about the world around them, not just repeat the clichés of the old masters. They looked to science as a model for art, believing that each motif and carving should be meticulously studied from nature, yet at the same time have something of the artist about it. Eventually, through the likes of Dante Gabriel Rossetti, virtually all of the major luminaries of the British Pre-Raphaelite movement were involved at some point in contributing to the decoration of the museum. They worked closely with the architects, masons and scientists

Figure 7.1 John Ruskin was able to put many of his ideas about nature and architecture into practice in the design of the Oxford Museum of Natural History, along with a number of eminent Pre-Raphaelite artists

Source: Photograph by Laurie Byrne on Unsplash.

to create a building that is in itself an artistic work of natural precision. A perfect example of this was the delightfully vivid stonework depicting all manner of flora and fauna in detail by the largely unsung O'Shea brothers, John and James. Ruskin himself drew several designs for windows on the façade carved by James O'Shea. However, much of the research and writing done about Ruskin's involvement in the Oxford Museum focuses on the architecture and little on the galleries and visitor experience itself. Where we see Ruskin's beliefs truly implemented in a museological sense is in Sheffield.

The Guild of St George

Ruskin's most deliberate and thorough foray into the world of museums came in Sheffield. The dehumanising and degrading conditions of industrial Britain and their negative effects on the human spirit was never far from Ruskin's mind. He was also conscious that the opportunities for observing beautiful places and objects through travel was not within the reach of the majority of people. His answer was to set up the Guild of St George, a philanthropic society through which Ruskin went on to establish a museum specifically for Sheffield's workers in Walkley in 1875.

He filled this museum with a collection of manuscripts, minerals, water-colours and drawings to reveal connections between nature and art, and to encourage the inventiveness of the city's craftsmen and women. The images depicted were often from his or other artists' travels and so he took his audience on imaginary journeys they could never hope to make physically. He even commissioned plaster castings of the capitals of the ducal Palace in Venice and carvings on French churches for the museum, the closest many working people would ever get to these works of art by Italian and French craftsmen. He expressly wanted to share his exploration of beauty with ordinary working people, not in a high-minded, academic way but in order to inspire happiness and well-being through an appreciation of a new way of looking at the world around them.

In this way, Ruskin displayed his faith in the inner life of the "uneducated" working classes. These were not collections meant for an elite class of connoisseurs but visual tools to be used for inspiration and betterment for the working man and woman. And this was no mere static collection, an impressive programme of engagement (such a buzzword in modern museums) which included lectures to reach out to the local community brought new audiences through the doors. In this sense, working-class men, women and children were able to "experience" the collection, each in their own way. This was a working example of Ruskin's most famous quote "there is no wealth but life" but which goes on "that country is richest which nourishes the greatest number of noble and happy human beings". One might say that he was championing the working-class right to "an inner life". Free of charge from its inception, the Ruskin Collection, still owned by the Guild of St George, is now housed at the Millennium Gallery in the city and is the focus of a programme of 'Ruskin in Sheffield' events.

Box 7.1 Case study 7: The 'Ruskin in Sheffield' project

A great example of Ruskin's philosophy in action in the present day is the 'Ruskin in Sheffield' project begun in 2013. The Guild of St George (keepers of the Ruskin flame) wanted to revive the connection between his collection and the people of Sheffield. They created this six-year, community-led, creative programme of events which included activities such as drawing in nature, discussions about the nature of wealth and devising better policies. Sixty community, culture groups and individuals participated across 76 , events, the majority of which were free, between 2014 and 2019, involving 150 professional artists and volunteers reaching an audience of over 25,000 (Nutter, 2020).

For six months a pop-up Ruskin Museum encouraged people to keep coming back through its community-based content and activities helping visitors to actively learn about their local heritage. The museum was run by a core group of specially recruited local volunteers who were involved in everything from sourcing furniture to initiating and hosting events. The museum evolved and grew through local visitor participation, attracting around 2,000 visitors. Local residents soon realised that they could use the space to initiate their own projects, including art shows, poetry readings and writing workshops. In another engagement exercise, a mobile structure designed by graduate architecture students of the University of Sheffield appeared on one of the city's busiest shopping streets. This created a space in which passers-by could engage in activities with professional craftspeople, hammering out metal bowls, weaving fabric bowls, carving wood or creating mini-mosaic sculptures. It was a place where all ages and walks of life mixed to exchange ideas, with older people particularly keen to share their knowledge of domestic and industrial skills. A "People's Palace of Possibility" created a theatrical space of discussion and ideas-sharing for visitors to contribute to creating policies and proposals for utopias in an open-minded and playful environment.

The over-riding spirit in which these projects were conducted was expressed by Ruth Nutter (2020), producer of the events programme:

> Building community is an open-ended process. It's not about imposing ideas or change on people, or trying to reach a specific endpoint. It's about being amongst people, listening, enabling, being curious, being active together, reflecting, retracing steps, changing track, being in a better place than when you started.

In commissioning these programmes, a number of guiding principles, inspired by John Ruskin's interconnected worldview, were used and developed which can be applied to planning community engagement projects more widely:

- *Purpose from passion:* the starting point for connecting with any local community must be rooted in your organisation's passion to connect and learn
- *Go polymath:* you need to offer a wide range of ways for people to come together and join in activities

- *Protest to prosper:* being together in safe spaces helps to build the habit of discussing what matters to people, even when they don't agree
- *Preserve and pioneer:* local heritage matters and can be a powerful driver for shaping the future
- *Paradise is here:* what if we focused our efforts on making paradise a place where we live?

Alongside these guiding principles a series of good practices were devised and evolved out of the lessons from the programmes and activities themselves, including:

- *Our place:* conversations need to be rooted in local communities
- *Very public places:* being highly visible attracts people but also allows people to feel safe and normalises the idea of people talking and participating
- *Pop-up:* unexpected appearances in public places are a powerful way of engaging people and gives people permission to act and think differently
- *Plenty of paper:* creativity aids communication so have plenty of materials available to help people express themselves
- *Putting it simply:* strike a simple, direct, non-jargony tone in your communications. This encourages people to take part and respond
- *In partnership:* building community collaboration, co-ownership, co-creation and co-production requires partnerships that recognise everyone's potential and actual contribution
- *Personal with people:* have a caring mindset in the way you approach people
- *Plan patiently:* allow plenty of time (a minimum of six months) to plan the events and partnerships that will form your community programme

Ruskin's legacy

The Oxford Museum of Natural History, the Ruskin Collection, the Guild of St George and events such as 'Ruskin in Sheffield' are all tangible results of Ruskin's philosophy and work. It is impossible to quantify the very real joy and improvement to the quality of life of the many ordinary working people that came into his orbit, whose eyes were opened to "learn to look". One can hazard a guess that the numbers over his long life were not inconsiderable.

However, Hanley and Walton (2010) convincingly argue that John Ruskin's influence on the field of tourism has been woefully neglected due to it so often being seen as a branch of business studies rather than cultural studies. Certainly, when one considers the wealth of material from Ruskin which can be said to include some aspect of tourism – from the "Stones of Venice" to the setting up of local tourism assets such as museums to his more esoteric advocacy of what might be termed a "touristic gaze"– his omission as a central figure in 19th-century British and European tourist history seems glaring. His Romantic anti-capitalism, which by its very nature resisted the idea of commodification, may well be the root of this glaring omission.

Ironically, at the end of his life the reclusive Ruskin became a tourist attraction himself, with people taking the train to the Lake District to try to get close to the man, or failing that to buy a postcard outside Brantwood, his home overlooking Coniston Water. There can be no doubt that Ruskin's generous spirit of inquiry and practical explorations of the wonder of beauty underpin, even if unconsciously, much that the museum and heritage industry tries to achieve today. Certainly, I detect his philosophy of egalitarian mischief and openness in the work of one of the next century's greatest exhibition designers, James Gardner, who we will discuss in the next chapter.

Conclusion

The polymath John Ruskin is what we would now call a "thought leader" of Victorian England. For him, the spiritual contemplation of art and architecture was at the heart of what it means to be human. He saw in the Gothic style in particular an antidote to what he regarded as the dehumanising predations of industrialisation and capitalism. However, his concerns were not only backward-looking as he championed contemporary British painters, such as J.M.W. Turner, and Gothic revivalism in the architecture of the day. In Ruskin's view, disconnecting the craftsman from his work was almost akin to a sin, and this desire for connection was a key influence that he brought to the field of heritage tourism; touching the chisel mark on a medieval arch was like shaking hands with the mason who carved it. Nor was the appreciation of the aesthetic an elitist pursuit, but one which Ruskin felt belonged to everyone; he credited ordinary people with an inner life worth nurturing. To this end, Ruskin took practical steps to foster an awareness and practice

134 *John Ruskin*

of art for the general public through the creation of a drawing school and museums, working closely with members of the Pre-Raphaelite movement. One could almost say that he invented the idea of the "touristic gaze" and was one of the world's foremost advocates of "learning to look".

References

Cook, E. & Wedderburn, A. (1904). *The works of John Ruskin.* Cambridge: Cambridge University Press.

Hanley, K. & Walton, J.K. (2010). *Constructing cultural tourism: John Ruskin and the tourist gaze.* Bristol: Channel View Publications.

Howard, P. (2003). *Heritage: management, interpretation, identity.* London: Continuum.

Nutter, R. (2020). *Paradise is here: building community around things that matter.* Sheffield: Guild of St George.

Ruskin, J. (1843). *Modern painters, Volume* I. London: Smith, Elder & Co.

Ruskin, J. (1851). *The stones of Venice.* New York: John Wiley.

Timothy, D.J. (2011). *Cultural and heritage tourism: an introduction.* Bristol: Channel View.

Further reading

Nutter, R. (2020). *Paradise is here: building community around things that matter.* Sheffield: Guild of St George.

Ruskin, J. (2004). *John Ruskin selected writings.* Oxford: Oxford University Press.

8   James Gardner

Interacting to learn

"Everything grows from something that grew before ..."

Narrative design in museum exhibitions has been a buzzword for well over a decade now. But sometimes it is paid lip service to, still being subordinated to the fetishisation of the artefact, to elitist concerns of connoisseurship or to the gimmicky use of the latest technology. So, it is instructive to trace the idea of narrative design in exhibitions back to its roots, back to a time when it was a radical approach, back to the originator of exhibitions as interactive experiences in which to learn – James Gardner.

James Gardner (1907–1995) was one of Britain's most important and influential post-war designers; yet he is also relatively little known outside of the academic realm of exhibition design history. His autobiography *Elephants in the Attic* (1983) paints a portrait of a studiedly carefree but sensitive and highly creative polymath, a trait he shared with John Ruskin (see Chapter 7). Uninterested in much that his local council school had to offer, Gardner found his first recognition for drawing when on a wet afternoon he stood on the touchline drawing his fellow pupils at games. Despite being reprimanded by the headmaster, the resulting sketch was hung in the school corridor and the 300 pupils were allowed to visit it three at a time. He experienced tragedy in his early teens when his mother died. His father soon remarried someone with whom Gardner clearly did not get on terribly well as he soon decamped for "seething London". There, he attended the Westminster School of Art whose alumni included artists such as Aubrey Beardsley, Eric Gill and Ethel Walker, and where Walter Sickert had been an influential teacher until 1918.

On graduating in 1923 at the tender age of 15, he began "the job that became his life", beginning as a commercial artist with Cartier

DOI: 10.4324/9781003369240-12

the jewellers of Bond Street London. At Cartier's drawing office, he soon learned that designers were not expected to conjure beauty from a void: "Everything grows from something that grew before, and the room contained a library of things that had gone before: Chinese carpets, Celtic bronze-work, Japanese sword hilts, Arabesques – designed to delight Emperors, Samurai and Kalifs"

(Gardiner, 1983)

Jacques Cartier himself would frequently demonstrate the essential vitality of design by breaking off from dealing with a rich customer to discuss the purpose and intention of a curve with the callow apprentice designer. The meaning of line became the meaning of life. However, he soon tired of "designing costly halters for the necks of status seekers' wives" and set off on a "tramp" to Africa with new boots bought at great expense from Jermyn Street.

On Gardner's return in 1931, he began working with what he regarded as the best commercial studio in Europe – Carlton Studios based in Great Queen Street. Founded in 1902 and run by Canadian artists Archibald Martin, T.G. Greene, Norman Mills Price, William Wallace

Figure 8.1 Portrait of James Gardner (no date). Cat. No: DCA-30–1-POR-G-4–1
Source: Design Council Archive, University of Brighton Design Archives.

and J.E.H. MacDonald, it produced illustrations and advertising graphics for a wide range of clients including Sandeman's Port, Boots the Chemists, State Express cigarettes and *Woman's Own*. It is here that he gained the sobriquet that stayed with him for the rest of his life – "G". He expressed the camaraderie of the practice as follows: "Carlton was us. If a gaggle of do-it-yourself specialists, who saw the world in terms of line, half-tone, or wash could be considered as having a 'corporate image' (an expression not yet coined)" (Gardiner, 1993).

In a word, Gardner and his colleagues were interested in technique. It was during this time that G began to produce some of his most enduring images and a lifelong love affair with transport technology when he visited the Short Brothers in Rochester to draw *The Canopus,* a yet unbuilt flying boat. A number of these cut-away illustrations showing the on-board facilities and technical innovations appeared on Imperial Airways advertising posters in the mid- to late 1930s, and still fetch good prices in London's Bond Street galleries.

The game of objects linked to ideas

This aeronautical connection was to prove fateful for both Gardner and the world of museums. Jack Beddington, director of publicity for Shell-Mex and BP, was known for his daring marketing stunts. The story about how Beddington gave Gardner his first exhibition design Commission is worth repeating verbatim:

> One day when I turned up with designs for a poster I found him in an angry mood, glaring at a thick manuscript on his desk. "Do you see this Gardner? I ask a top aeronautical consultant to prepare a script for an exhibition and what do I get? A book." He flipped the pages testily. "It's textbook material; The man's a fool." He then looked up and observed me appraisingly. "It's for an exhibition about how aircraft fly. Do you know how they fly?" I said I thought so. "Do you know what I mean by the word exhibition?" I said yes, I'd visited some. "Well, then see what you can make of it."
>
> (Gardner, 1983)

One could say that it was at this moment, in the mid-1930s, that the modern interpretive exhibition design industry was born. Gardner promised to deliver a treatment for the exhibition in three days; and so we can also say that the tendency towards over-optimistic exhibition design deadlines was born simultaneously. Typically, Gardner was ahead of the game having spent the past few months researching the topic out of interest and holding a glider pilot's licence himself. He delivered an immaculate proposal on time.

Gardner's reflections on first entering the world of exhibitions are instructive. Those he had seen to date he viewed as very ordinary. When draughting his drawings into 3-D, he tried to make every exhibit "pretty, ingenious, or in some way out of the ordinary". He used people's natural sense of curiosity as the motivation to explore the exhibition and played what he called the "game of objects linked to ideas".

Chief Development Officer, Camouflage

Gardner's connection with Beddington led to his next career move and it was in a rather unexpected direction. But then war does that. Beddington had influence at the War Office and was appointed head of the Ministry of Information Films Division in April 1940. To the credit of Britain's wartime establishment, Gardner's peculiar creative talents were put to full use to confuse Hitler's armed forces in a newly formed special camouflage unit. So began an episode in Gardner's life that would not have looked out of place in Evelyn Waugh's "Sword of Honour" trilogy. Blimpish colonels presided over a ragtag of conscripted artists, magicians, designers and bird watchers to come up with ever more outlandish camouflage schemes to outwit a fiendishly clever enemy.

It wasn't just about designing ways of concealing military hardware or troops. Credible, accurate models or inflatable stand-ins for real military equipment had to be accurately designed, alongside the dark arts of misinformation. In one instance, Gardner helped design an entirely new (and as it turned out fictitious) type of British tank in order to waste the enemy's valuable intelligence time and effort. Not only did the tank have to be believable enough in technical terms, but it also needed a believable back story. Bogus but detailed technical blueprints were drawn up and aerial photos of fake assembly areas complete with tank tracks and camouflage nets draped over mysterious tank-like lumps were created. Gardner dubbed himself Chief Development Officer, Camouflage. Not all his inventions were so innocuous; a replica German bicycle pump issued to the French Resistance "blew quite a number of German officers' arms off". As D-Day for the re-invasion of Europe approached the need to create diversionary "forces" to keep the enemy guessing where the true landing force might embark from became ever-more important. Gardner produced a whole catalogue of inflatable dummy equipment with which he could virtually overnight conjure an impressive mass of supposed hardware that would keep the Germans' reconnaissance efforts guessing. So successful were the deception tactics employed by Gardner and his unit that Churchill said that their "final result was admirable". Museum exhibition designers should be in no doubt as to how this "smoke and mirrors" approach to design is relevant.

Britain Can Make It

No sooner had the Second World War ended than Gardner's old patron Jack Beddington pointed him in the direction of no less a person than Sir Stafford Cripps, Chancellor of the Exchequer, who wanted to invoke a spirit of optimism by exhibiting gadgets of the future at the then empty Victoria and Albert (V&A) Museum. The Council of Industrial Design were to select the consumer goods they thought would have most impact on people's lives in the future and Gardner was tasked with designing "a setting that would give the public a lift even if we got no goods at all". He had moved from Spitfires to saucepans.

Britain Can Make It was the first exhibition in post-war-torn Europe, and quite possibly the world. Without the V&A's usual displays, which had been hidden in the countryside to avoid the bombing of London, Gardner had the whole ground floor of the Exhibition Road site to play with. He set about trying to solve a problem that faces exhibition designers surprisingly often today: how to design an exhibition that will look complete in every detail even if there are no objects to display? He did this by devising a new kind of layout, one in which, rather than creating a shop window of objects, exhibits were concealed around corners to draw visitors through the exhibition via a series of surprises. It proved so successful that this technique became a well-used tool in his museum design toolbox. He also introduced an element of theatricality by dressing the formal marble halls with tented drapes and perfuming the air in the women's fashion section. It was certainly a change from the drab khaki-filled world of war. It also proved to be a baptism of fire, a crash course in what it takes to devise and choreograph the installation of one of the most complex types of design. For the first time in a museum exhibition context, Gardner, rather than go it alone, had to learn how to delegate to his team of strong-willed designers, deal with the unionisation of artists and coordinate five know-it-all contractors. Opened by King George VI in 1946, the exhibition was a success and a year later Gardner opened his own office with what was left of the fee.

The Festival of Britain

As soon as Gardner had established his company at London Mayfair's 13 Duke Street, he encountered the familiar cashflow issues that dog almost all design companies: "aiming to get paid for Job A before we had spent it all working on Job B, the money for which would cover expenses already committed to Job C". Consequently, he took on any work that came his way, but especially trade exhibitions. The international future that his company was destined for was foreshadowed by work for R.D. Tata, whose company was already a massive conglomerate of industries in India. It was soon after this that he received the commission that would place Gardner's work on the national stage – the Festival of Britain.

In the spirit of post-war renaissance, it was decided that what the country needed was a huge celebration of all things British on the centenary of Prince Albert's Great Exhibition of 1851. The site chosen was to leave a legacy that is known to all Londoners as the South Bank. Hugh Casson and Gardner were given the downstream area on the theme of "living" to "create a little golden world of hope". Gardner was also appointed to design the Pleasure Gardens in Battersea. Much trial and tribulation followed, but Gardner deemed it all a success when, rather than a royal opening, the first person to pass through the turnstiles was "one of the millions of us ordinaries the show had been designed for" and on the last night after a firework display groups of "ordinaries" were doing "Knees Up Mother Brown", singing and cheering. That this should be his measure of success for such a patriotically prestigious project points to Gardner's subversive sense of egalitarianism.

The designer of global Britain

Gardner's success at projecting an image of modern Britishness led to him being given not just the design but the theme, research, budgeting and production of the national pavilion at the World Fair (or Expo) in Brussels in 1958. The UK Pavilion went on to win the gold medal, leading to him also designing the UK Travelling Exhibition in 1960. Despite Gardner's subversive streak he continued to be the chosen exhibition designer for The Establishment (he had, after all, also designed the public decorations for the Queen's coronation in 1953). Work for the Commonwealth Institute (CI) in 1962 required Gardner to devise displays for the various nations that made up the Commonwealth. These exhibition "courts" were dedicated to the cultural, economic and political histories, as well as contemporary agendas, of each country. The archive of James Gardner's work is now held by the University of Brighton Design Archives and, 50 years after the event, its Dr Claire Wintle described her first reaction in coming across his sketches for the CI dioramas: "In their dynamic, highly coloured rendering, and in their

Figure 8.2 Proposed Ceylon Court, Commonwealth Institute, London, 1961. Cat.
No: LJG-3-3-2–18
Source: James Gardner Archive, University of Brighton Design Archives.

very existence, the sketches themselves challenged my own stereotypes of
what I had imagined mid-century British exhibitions of empire and
commonwealth to look like."

Two projects – the QE2 and Evoluon – completed in the mid-1960s
crystallised Gardner's position in British design as both an aesthetic
interpreter of British identity and a pioneer of global exhibition design.
When the UK government decided in the early 1960s to loan Cunard the
money to create a new ocean liner it was suggested by Jim Fitton, an
advisor to the company's advertising agency, that a designer from outside the maritime field might be a good idea. Gardner was approached
and, after a typically insouciant insistence that the only ship he had ever
designed was a showboat for the amusement park at Battersea, was duly
appointed as the designer of the above water lines, including the profile
of the ocean liner. The QE2 was to become an icon of British maritime
history, topped off with an innovative funnel design. Having designed a
far more streamlined superstructure profile of the "block of utility flats
dumped at sea" than that he first encountered on entering Cunard's
drawing office, there needed to be a similar revolution in terms of its
business model in order to keep the QE2 afloat commercially. The way
the passengers used Gardner's contemporary interiors of the liner needed
to be thought through as much as its timeless profile. In 1968, she was
launched into the Clyde and ocean liner history was made.

Evoluon and the invention of interactivity

Opened in 1966, the use of the Evoluon "flying saucer" for a series of concerts by popular German electro band Kraftwerk in 2013 is testament to its iconic place in design futurism. Now a conference centre, this UFO poised over a lake in Eindhoven was designed "to shoehorn the people of the Netherlands into the twentieth century" by showing them how technology is the driver of modern society as part of Philips' 75th anniversary. This was to be done by means of a science museum looking at cutting edge topics such as nuclear physics, genetics and human perception. Wading through technical committees of content experts, Gardner became increasingly aware of how challenging it is to make the complicated seem simple through an exhibit, as well as the complexity of museum design itself: "The first 40ft run of exhibits has involved mechanics, film projection, modeling, artwork and going back to one's childhood .... The program is inexpressibly complicated, but the job must look very simple when completed."

And it was Evoluon that brought Gardner more fully into the world of interactive exhibitry:

> A visitor who had just arrived is content to stand and stare, but soon he will itch to fiddle. I must introduce games, or what for want of a better name I term quizzes, what museologists would refer to as visitor participation. These can be costly – and chancy – affairs.

The Evoluon proved to be extremely popular, attracting over 500,000 visitors in 1970 alone, primarily due to its thought-provoking interactive exhibits. As such, it is a major landmark in the development of science and technology exhibitions. There was probably not a more successful or ground-breaking permanent science museum until the development of the San Francisco's Exploratorium by former atomic scientist Frank Oppenheimer which opened in 1969. Indeed, the Exploratorium is often cited as the paradigm for science centres thereafter but Alex McCuaig, Gardner's protégé and a world-renowned museum designer himself (see Chapter 9), thinks otherwise:

> I think Gardner was the first guy ever to let you be engaged in the interactivity of a museum's storyline, rather than be a passive observer. He was the first man to do that, I think. This was way before the Exploratorium. Oppenheimer took what Gardner had done and put it into an American culture.

Gardner's work on another science museum, the "Story of the Earth" at London's Geological Museum in 1972, where he had produced an exciting show "given only heaps of rocks and a few tectonic charts", led to him being contacted by Karl Katz of the Metropolitan Museum in New York for a project that was eventually to be called the "Museum of the Jewish Diaspora" in Tel Aviv. Based around the central aspects of Jewish life (family, community, faith, culture, existence and return), it was intended to fill in the gaps of history between ancient Jewish history and the most recent Six-Day War. When it opened in 1978, it quickly took its place as one of the world's best and most technologically advanced museums, breaking the mould of museums' primary task of being to acquire, collect and conserve rather than tell stories in the most effective way possible.

It was in this same year that James Gardner (3-D Concepts) Ltd was formed. Through this company he would nurture a number of museum designers who themselves have gone on to forge a name for themselves in the industry. One of the first specialist museum design companies in the UK, it developed projects from concept through to supervising installation. The Tel Aviv project led to other gallery work for Jewish heritage organisations such as the Tower of David Museum, Jerusalem (1989) and the Museum of Tolerance, Los Angeles (1993). However, it was his work for the National Museum of Natural Science (NMNS) in Taichung, Taiwan where I first encountered Gardner's work professionally when I began working at Alex McCuaig's company, MET Studio Ltd in 1992.

Box 8.1 Case study 8: National Museum of Natural Science (NMNS), Taiwan

The founding Director of the NMNS in Taiwan, Dr Pao-teh Han, had a vision for the museum that would combine "the elegances of the natural world with the beauty of art". He felt that James Gardner was the right designer to help him achieve this vision and, following his first visit to his offices, Dr Han left a wonderfully evocative description of Gardner and his working style:

> When I entered his Studio I felt that I had already found the man I was looking for. The place was not the slick interior designers normally opt for, but a domain of fantasy. The mannequin of a Victorian parlour maid stood by a window, a faint light shines on a miniature Southern Song Dynasty cup, and the place was full of things he had designed, from works of art to strange devices,

a wire model for a robot, a working steam engine, and ships. In his early 80s, Gardner has white hair and bright eyes, a designer with a free spirit. A brilliant conversationalist, he immediately addressed me by my name and I felt suddenly uplifted.

We can hear echoes from this description of Cartier's "library of things" where Gardner had started out all those decades before.

Gardner's plan was to make the NMNS the first museum in the world which would explain how life on Earth evolved in a continuous sequence from its start to ardnerthe present. It was part of a huge museum building masterplan by the government of Taiwan which saw education as a key advantage in modernising their economy. He was told that the museum-going public of Taiwan were not terribly sophisticated and had short attention spans. This would necessitate him bringing out every trick in the museum designer's manual for the 17 galleries he was to design, including going back to Victorian techniques such as large, modelled dioramas.

The museum was opened in four phases from 1986 to 1999: firstly, the Science Centre and Space IMAX Theater; then the Life Science Hall; followed by the Human Cultures Hall; and finally the Global Environment Hall, including the Bird's-Eye View Theater, Environment Theater and 3D Theater. The Science Centre and Space IMAX Theater were a clever taster to convey the mix of entertainment and education that would characterise the NMNS at the museum entrance. The Human Cultures Hall promotes the contribution of China to sciences, culture and civilisation relying heavily on the works of the likes of Joseph Needham. The Global Environment Hall depicted the close relationship between ecology and the environment by depicting whole ecosystems and the interdependence of species within them. For instance, a walkthrough experience of a Costa Rican rainforest allowed visitors to call up species on computer terminals along the route (which sounds basic now but was revolutionary at the time) and had reproductions of plants of which moulds had been taken in situ on a field trip by the production team. Features like the audiovisual theatres were in some cases bespoke, standalone specialist spaces. I experienced the working prototype of the Environment Theatre in London, for instance, before it was dismantled to be shipped to Taiwan for reassembly. It was the production for these galleries that, in Gardner's words, was "activated by Alex, an ex-assistant with an abrasive Scottish accent, effective when troubleshooting". This was Alex McCuaig who founded MET

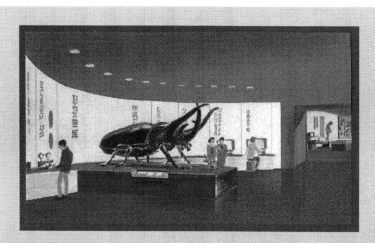

Figure 8.3 View of a section of the interior with a giant beetle exhibit, National Museum of Natural Science, Taiwan, 1986–1988. Cat. No: LJG-3–22-2-6
Source: James Gardner Archive, University of Brighton Design Archives.

Studio in 1982 and two years later took on the responsibility of supervising the installation of an entire museum designed by Gardner for the NMNS.

The last major museum designed by James Gardner, the Museum of Tolerance, opened in 1993 in Los Angeles. As the educational arm of the Simon Wiesenthal Center, it is dedicated to challenging visitors to understand the Holocaust in both historic and contemporary contexts, and confront all forms of prejudice and discrimination in our world today. It soon received acclaim from national and international leaders, and was described by newspapers and magazines worldwide as an extraordinary new museum. It became a "must-see" attraction in Southern California and has since been visited by over five million visitors, mostly middle- and high-school students.

James Gardner passed away in 1995. The archive of his work and personal papers is held by the University of Brighton Design Archives which describes him as "one of Britain's most imaginative post-war designers". Alex McCuaig had over 40 years' connection with Gardner both personally and professionally and summed up his approach to museum design as follows:

Many design companies had a house style which they would work up. Gardner worked from the other direction. He worked from "What is the subject?". What research do we need to do to compile a narrative? How do we translate that narrative into something real? Something 3-dimensional, 2-dimensional, and reaches the visitor in a really exciting storyline, something that they would be engaged in. Gardner's museums were like a good book in the sense that you start off getting into it, you start to understand how to use it and before you know it you're engaged, engulfed. You don't want to put it down until you read it, got through it. His attitude was to develop the job up from the roots. Design came later.

We will look at how Gardner's legacy has been continued through the career of Alex McCuaig in the Chapter 9.

Conclusion

James Gardner was a global pioneer of narrative design for more than half a century. Despite being one of Britain's most prolific and influential post-war designers, he is little known outside of academia. Beginning as a commercial advertising artist, he was by chance given an opportunity to design an exhibition on aeronautics in the mid-1930s. One could argue that this marked the beginning of the modern interpretive exhibition design industry. The intervention of the Second World War saw Gardner involved in the tragi-comedy of Britain's deceptive camouflage unit, where he learned the optical tricks and illusions that would stand him in good stead for a career in museum design. James Gardner had an almost Ruskinesque faith in the general public's innate sense of curiosity; once he had piqued a visitor's interest he could lead them on a journey of discovery through his exhibition galleries. He was able to project his early success in British museums and visitor experiences onto the global stage, almost single-handedly creating the international market for the specialist museum design industry. And key to this success was his ability to arouse a sense of curiosity in his visitors through the extensive and innovative use of interactive exhibits: interacting to learn.

References and further reading

Gardiner, J. (1983). *Elephants in the attic*. London: Orbis Publishing.
Gardiner, J. (1993). *The ARTful designer*. London: Centurion Press.

9   Alex McCuaig

Experiencing to inspire

Standing on the shoulders of giants

As founder of MET Studio (MET), Alex McCuaig has been at the fore-front of museum and exhibition design for over 40 years. As we have seen in the previous chapter, he was a protégé of James Gardner whose work is now held by the University of Brighton Design Archives as an important resource for the history of post-war exhibition design. In 2016, at the FX International Design Awards, McCuaig was presented with the Outstanding Lifetime Contribution to Design Award for the impact of the educational, cultural and immersive experiences he has created over this period. In the same year, one of MET's projects won *Wired* magazine's Age of Design Award as the best piece of design in 25 years, beating the likes of Apple's original iPhone. Looking at case studies from MET's portfolio over four decades and through conversations with McCuaig himself himself (quotes in this chapter derive from these), we aim in this chapter to present a critical account of the evolution of museum and exhibition design from the early 1980s to the present day through the prism of one design company.

Down the slipway

On 20 September 1967 at John Brown's shipyard on the Clyde, Queen Elizabeth II (1926–2022) spoke the somewhat self-referential words: "I name this ship Queen Elizabeth the Second." Some accounts, possibly apocryphal, state that in fact the addition of "the Second" was made by the Queen herself. In the end, the numeral 2 was used instead of the Roman II, presumably to appear more hip in the swinging sixties. So big was she (the ship, not the Queen) that her bow overhung the slipway. As we have seen in the last chapter, James Gardner was the designer of the "sleek, modern and purposeful" superstructure and profile (according to

DOI: 10.4324/9781003369240-13

the Council of Industrial Design at the time), as well as the interiors. Once the champagne bottle had shattered on her hull, the immense structure glided down to meet the sea "through a cloud of rust-dust from the drag chains, she [sent] a wave down the Clyde as though a glacier has calved an iceberg" (Gardner, 1993). This momentous occasion was witnessed by a 16-year old called Alex McCuaig who had not yet decided on a career:

> My relationship with Gardner started before I knew him. It started when I saw the QE2 on its maiden voyage after its launch sailing down the Clyde. That, to me, is almost spooky. That was the first thing in my life that I actually realised was a beautiful piece of design.

Not that seeing the QE2 gliding down the Clyde resulted in McCuaig immediately jumping onto the slipway to become a museum designer. For one thing, he was not aware of museum design as a profession, nor of any such college course existing at that time; it was beyond his ken. So, despite this serendipitous brush with "G" ("Not G for God, but G for Gardner. Although he used to think he was God at times"), it was pure luck that McCuaig ended up in museum design.

On leaving Helensburgh's Hermitage Academy Secondary School, McCuaig struck out for London in 1969. There, he worked in the building industry before going to Goldsmiths (University of London) and then graduating from Kingston Polytechnic (now University) as a mature student in 1978. Fortune intervened when a colleague of Gardner's spotted McCuaig's work at the end of year graduation show. He was invited to meet Gardner who saw the potential in his portfolio and offered him a job on £4,500 per year. It was at this point that McCuaig decided to find out who this man was and discovered Gardner's connection with the QE2; that was the "clincher" that made McCuaig want to go to work for him:

> James Gardner was already working worldwide when most museum designers were trapped in the UK working with national museums that were a bit didactic and working with parochial museums around the country. Gardner just went out and started working worldwide. He could see a much bigger marketplace and work in cultures where others feared to tread. It certainly taught me that you should go and work overseas to get a global cultural understanding of the differences in people that allow you to develop museum projects that were geared for that audience and not just rolling out projects using the same formula.

Towards commercial independence

The first museum that McCuaig worked on for Gardner was the Evo-luon, the Philips Museum, in Eindhoven. He soon came to realise that one of the things that set Gardner apart from other designers was that, yes, he did projects which had the express intention of educating, but he did this with a light-hearted touch and without a sense of elitism. He believes Gardner was the first designer to come up with a new paradigm for museums of being both educational and entertaining for a much wider audience. Two years after leaving university, whilst working on the Science Museum in Baltimore, McCuaig got experience meeting with senators and senior executives at board meetings of the Baltimore Gas and Electric. Gardner gave him the opportunity and confidence to deal with people "way out of my league". This was a fast-track experience which greatly accelerated his passage to commercial independence.

Another important lesson that McCuaig learned from Gardner was how a collaborative process gets a better end result. This collaboration came in many forms – from local artisans to root the project in the community to other partners in the design industry. Bringing in artists to manufacture exhibits or working with audiovisual producers, whilst commonplace in museum projects now, was not widely done in the museum world at that time. And in the ego-driven world of design (and I can speak from personal experience on this), a genuine, open-minded willingness to collaborate and overcome barriers of petty jealousies is a rare thing.

At this time, the artefact was still king and the keepers of the arte-facts, emperors. However, McCuaig also learned that museums did not necessarily need collections - they were there to tell stories. Gardner's 29,000-square-metre National Museum of Natural Science (NMNS) in Taiwan, commissioned by the visionary museum director Dr Pao-teh Han (see Chapter 8), was designed with only one single artefact (a Chi-nese dragon robe) quite simply because there were none. Instead, the museum takes the visitor on an experiential journey through the story of evolution and the wonders of the natural world. Again, this may be par for the course for many science museums now but back in the 1980s it was a radical departure. This non-elitist approach opened up museums to a much wider audience around the world. The NMNS is now in the top 20 museums visited in the world (one behind the Musée d'Orsay in Paris) according to the European museums network.

Having worked with Glaswegians on the QE2 at John Brown's ship-yard, Gardner had faith in their ability to get things done which exten-ded to sending this assistant with "an abrasive Scottish accent" all over the world to troubleshoot on his projects. After working for 4½ years with Gardner, McCuaig felt he had the confidence to set up on his own, sensing that he had already learned all he needed to know from "the master": "I learned to have confidence in working with almost anybody – from government ministers to corporate organisations .... I learned almost everything I know from my mentor, James Gardner."

In setting up his new company, McCuaig took something else from his time with Britain's most prolific and successful post-war public designer: the lack of need for a "house style" for his company. Rather, in 1982, McCuaig instilled in his newly formed company MET Studio Ltd (named after his first studio location on the banks of the Thames in London – the Metropolitan Wharf) the philosophy of rooting any design in the content of the exhibition or museum through a well-researched narrative: "Gardner's museums were like a good book; before you knew it you were engaged. His attitude was to develop a job up from the roots. Design came later." To this end, MET Studio was one of the few design companies in the field to consistently maintain a full-time research department staffed by researchers with a museum or academic background (which I myself joined in 1992 under the tutelage of Deirdre Janson-Smith, Director of Research).

Another influence of Gardner's approach to projects on McCuaig was his desire to push projects beyond the expectations of the client. This could sometimes be a risky approach that put pressure on the project budget but is undoubtedly responsible for some of the critically acclaimed outcomes for which MET has become known. Indeed, pushing the envelope of what could be done in visitor experiences became something of a MET Studio signature, to such an extent that one museum director said, "I love what MET Studio does but you're not going to do any experiments with my money." McCuaig's response was: "Then why did you engage us because that's what we're here to do." However big or small the project or budget MET Studio has always sought to push the envelope of what is possible in exhibition design, but within the boundaries of budget and client requirements. We will look at how this was done over a number of decades, territories and projects.

MET Studio is launched

In the same year that Michael Jackson released *Thriller* and Argentina invaded the Falkland Islands (or Malvinas depending on your persuasion), MET Studio was formed in London as a partnership (it did not become a limited company until 1996). Its core areas of business have remained consistent since that time: museums, exhibitions, international expos and corporate brand experiences. In its 40-plus year existence it has created projects in more than 50 countries and in founder Alex McCuaig's view storytelling has always been at the heart of what MET does:

> Although, at heart, we are a professional design studio, our day-to-day work encompasses so much more than that. We are storytellers, and we work with clients to tell their story across every step of an exhibit or project, from feasibility, market research and financing through to masterplanning, design and build.

The next few years were largely preoccupied with the installation supervision of James Gardner's 14 galleries of Phase II at the NMNS. The large number of individual exhibits (approximately 2,000) meant that the manpower of James Gardner's relatively small studio had to be supplemented by other companies for the detail design of the galleries, which McCuaig sourced including Ralph Applebaum Associates of New York, MET Studio and Brennan & Whalley of London.

The 1990s

The first major gallery commission in its own right of MET Studio came in the early 1990s when the Wellcome Trust commissioned the 550-square-metre, £1.6-million Science for Life gallery. It was around this time that I myself joined MET as a humble researcher. Science for Life was to be the main focus of the Wellcome Centre for Medical Science in London, a place where people could learn about the past, present and future of biomedical science and appreciate its impact on everyday life. The objective of Science for Life was to explain and celebrate biomedical science, explored the mysteries of the human body, the nature of scientific discovery and the work of the scientist. Perhaps one of the most overtly Gardner-influenced exhibitions in MET's portfolio, the exhibition cleverly incorporated innovative technology and beautifully designed exhibits to present life, its processes and discoveries in an entertaining and accessible way. For instance, a centrepiece of the gallery was a walkthrough experience of a human cell magnified a million times which allowed visitors to learn about the organelles and functions of a cell, as well as undergo an immersive interpretation of what happens when a cell is attacked by a virus. No less a person than Sir David Attenborough described Science for Life as "one of the most exciting and innovative exhibitions on science that you will find anywhere in this country" and it went on to win Best Exhibition Design at the Design Week Awards in 1994.

Around this time, by a twist of fate, MET were appointed as designers for the interior spaces and external livery of the QE2 for its 1994 refit entitled "Project Lifestyle". McCuaig's emotional links with Glasgow, the history of the ship and James Gardner no doubt helped persuade the Cunard board that he was the man for the job. Teamed with experienced marine interior designer John McNeece, MET undertook an extensive period of research into the customer experience and expectations to produce a masterplan that orchestrated the public spaces of the ship in line with the passengers' patterns of behaviour. It went on to design a number of public areas such as the Caronia Restaurant, Crystal Bar, Yacht Club, Chart Room, Queen's Room and Library, as well as the heart of the ship's passenger traffic the Midships Lobby.

A heritage trail acted as a navigational aid for passengers to find their way around providing museum-like moments and displaying original artefacts from the ship's and Cunard's history, such as a refurbished model of the Mauretania complete with internal lighting in tune with the day-night cycle. I myself remember pleasurable hours spent as a researcher at Ocean Pictures (who owned the rights to photos taken onboard) to select images for the trail. The company's museum experience was on display particularly in its appreciation of the ocean liner as a piece of iconic British heritage, but it also displayed a keen commercial sense of how to leverage aspirational nostalgia for profit. Currently docked in Dubai, the 1994 QE2 refit is perhaps the MET project that still receives the most comment on online forums devoted to the ship, the vast majority of it positive particularly regarding the Midships Lobby and heritage trail.

An example of how MET would push the envelope of audiovisual experiences even in those pre-digital days takes us back to Taiwan and the NMNS. Dubbed "an extraordinary and impressive experience" by *AV* magazine, the Environment Theatre was a 360-degree, multi-media environment which introduced visitors to the themes of the Museum's other galleries – inspiring them to go and make their own voyage of discovery. Visitors would sit on a revolving platform beneath an array of many (frankly quite noisy) slide projectors to experience one of three dynamic multi-media shows on a 7-metre-high cyclorama, with mechanical screens circulating and dropping down to create multi-layered tableaus. It was an impressive example of a pre-digital, analogue immersive experience which are so much easier to produce these days with digital audiovisual display technology.

Still in the Far East, a project that heralded MET's arrival in Hong Kong (a presence that was to eventually see a regional office set up and a continuing presence for more than 25 years) was the 3,000-square-metre

Figure 9.1 Alex McCuaig with the QE2's 21st Master from 2003–2008, Ian McNaught
Source: Photograph by Alex McCuaig.

Telecom World. Costing US$16 million and spread over three floors of Hongkong Telecom's offices in Quarry Bay, it was an ambitious and pioneering public access exhibition and marketing suite, a corporate experience communicating the science behind the company's activities in a comprehensible way. The exhibition was the world's first extensive use of smartcard technology in a major public exhibition, with visitors using a tailored card to access interactive exhibits in their own language and at their own age level. In recognition, it garnered the accolade of Best Exhibition at the 1996 Design Week Awards.

At the end of the 1990s, MET made a rare foray into the US market which saw the Underground Adventure at the storied Field Museum open in March 1999. It was the first ever outside consultancy commissioned for a project of this scope and value by one of America's oldest and most prestigious museums. The designers were tasked with increasing visitation to the museum through a permanent gallery about the most unpromising of subjects – soil. Taking an experiential approach unusual for formal museums at the time, McCuaig sold the vision to the Trustees of shrinking visitors to within one hundredth of their size, allowing them to walk through 6 inches of North American prairie soil and encounter the oversized creatures that live there on their way. By showing the incredible diversity of life in the soil and the importance of our connections to it, the exhibition offered a totally immersive, dynamic, entertaining and accessible experience on the most profoundly unglamorous of subjects. Underground Adventure, which was a ticketed exhibition, achieved 1,000,000 visitors in the first 16 months after opening. John W. Carter Jr, President of the Field Museum, praised the gallery's "imagination, creativity and overall thoughtfulness".

As the millennium drew to a close, MET produced one of its most award-winning projects to date and one which showed its bold approach to collaboration and the use of technology. Wired Worlds was the UK's first ever gallery dedicated to digital media as the centrepiece of the National Museum of Photography, Film and Television's (NMPFT) £16 million expansion programme. Working with the Museum's in-house team, MET "dispensed with traditional museum approaches and adopted a scheme based on a series of commissioned digital media artworks by practitioners whose work has largely been unseen by the general public in the UK" (Ferris, 2000). Just as James Gardner had worked with local artisans, the MET team worked with digital artists to illustrate a series of particular themes or messages within the space including Nigel Johnson (UK), Toshio Iwai (Japan), Art+Com (Germany), Paul Sermon (UK), Jane Prophet (UK) and Jeffrey Shaw (Australia). According to the NMPFT curator Malcolm Ferris, "For the artists, every installation had to walk a knife-edge – to uphold its claim as a work of art within the context of a museological space whose primary function is to inform in a critical yet entertaining manner." The gallery went on to win the Design Week Award for Best of Show and Best Exhibition at the DBA Design Effectiveness Awards in 2000, and in 2016 won *Wired* magazine's Age of Design Award as the best piece of design in 25 years, beating the likes of Apple's original iPhone and iPad, the BBC identity, the British Airways First-class seat and the Norton F1 motorcycle.

The 2000s

The emergence of what might be called the "Experience Economy" (Pine & Gilmore, 1999) in the run up to the millennium heralded a huge boost to the sector particularly with the UK government's injection of capital to fund celebratory projects. The largest landmark millennium project in England outside of London, Birmingham's Millennium Point, opened in Autumn 2001 and incorporated Thinktank. This housed galleries built around the collections of what was previously the Birmingham Museum of Science and Industry. MET was commissioned to masterplan the interior spaces and design four science-based galleries – Things About

Me, Wild Life, Medicine Matters and The Street/Science Around Us. These covered a wide range of topics from the science of objects that we use in our everyday lives, through to the migratory habits of birds and mammals. *FX* magazine judged that,

> MET Studio's four galleries take the museum experience to an even higher level of interaction ... Getting the public to leave their homes and pay money to come to these places is becoming increasingly difficult and museums designers are under ever more pressure to up the ante when designing the exhibitions. Luckily, we have designers who rise to the challenge.

In early 2000, MET received its biggest project to date in Hong Kong. The commission was to design what would be at that time the world's largest wetland park experience in the New Territories. This was intended to take tourism pressure off the adjoining Mai Po Inner Deep Bay Ramsar site, located as it is on an important migration route for birds coming from Russia and a stop-off point for many rare breeds, such as the spoonbill. The client was the Agricultural, Fisheries and Conservation Department (AFCD) of the Hong Kong government and the project was being run by the Architectural Services Department (ArchSD).

Masterplanning began in May 2000 and entailed undertaking a feasibility study with the ArchSD, consulting the various stakeholders (Tourism Department, Highways, Planning Department, etc.) and creating a series of Technical Reports and an Executive Summary that set out a Strategic Plan for the project. An architectural brief for the exhibition building and the 61 hectares of landscape was also outlined. MET then won the design services phase of all the public spaces, galleries and interpretation out in the natural reserves.

Working with the Wildfowl and Wetlands Trust (WWT), this resulted in the opening in 2006 of the Hong Kong Wetland Park (HKWP) – one of the world's most advanced wetland conservation, education and tourism facilities at the time consisting of a 10,000-square-metre visitor centre concealed beneath a mounded, sloping grass roof and a wild reserve consisting of a wide range of created habitats, including freshwater, brackish and inter-tidal wetlands, reedbed, grassland, mangrove, shrubland and woodlands. The approaches taken by the galleries were deliberately varied and demonstrated MET's range of experiential design philosophies. What are Wetlands? introduced the topic through hands-on, science-museum-like interactive exhibits that provided an overview of the functions and values of wetlands, the Ramsar Convention and the importance of wetlands to wildlife. "Living Wetlands" allowed visitors to explore three stylised environments via walkthrough dioramas – the Frozen North, Tropical Swamp (including a large aquarium housing live False Gharials) and Hong Kong Wetlands. The Human Culture gallery used a central audiovisual show around which were arranged mixed-media artefacts with audiovisual to convey how wetlands have always given us vital resources and how they are celebrated in all cultures across the world. Finally, the "Wetland Challenge" used a smartcard to allow visitors to act as a journalist investigating issues of wetland threat and conservation along an abstracted "river" that flows through the gallery. Cheung (2008) points to the success of the range of interpretive devices and presentations in attracting, particularly, domestic tourists to the HKWP, both promoting ecotourism and raising awareness of the need for wetland conservation.

While the HKWP was being designed, MET's success in the international museum design marketplace was recognised by the Queen's Award – a very rare accolade for any UK design company. The awards are recommended by a panel of experts reporting to the UK Prime Minister and then approved by the Queen before being conferred annually on the Queen's birthday (21 April) in recognition of outstanding business achievement. This came about after achieving a

Figure 9.2 The Hong Kong Wetland Park included a walkthrough swamp experience complete with live false gharials
Source: Photograph by MET Studio.

year-on-year increase in export revenue since the formation of the company, earning impressive overseas design fees for the three years to the end of December 2002, including from 16 separate commissions from clients in Hong Kong, China, Taiwan, Singapore, Germany, Ireland, Portugal, Spain and the US.

The 2010s

In the 2010s, MET returned to the Americas with a masterplan (produced as a joint venture collaboration with a specialist exhibition fabricator from the San Francisco Academy of Science) for the Museo de Ciencias Ambientales (Museum of Environmental Sciences), Guadalaja in Mexico. It then independently went on to be awarded the design of the galleries of the 14,000-square-metre engagement centre to explore themes of sustainability, ecosystems and man's interaction and impact on landscapes and agriculture, with a particular focus on the relationship between the city of Guadalajara and its natural and agricultural resources out into the state of Jalisco as far as the coast. A free-flow experience created a "living tapestry" of exhibits and activities with clear circulation, positioned content clusters, vistas and highlight exhibits, so that visitors could intuitively explore the three-dimensional immersive narrative.

Back in Europe, despite having access to one of the world's largest collections of maritime history at the Het Sheepvaartmuseum (the National Maritime Museum of the Netherlands), together with the client and Tinker exhibition content developers from Holland MET took the bold step of designing a series of three zones around just three objects: the 350-year-old museum building (a former naval depot) itself, a series of letters from an 18th-century sailor and a blanket in which a little girl was rescued from a sinking ship in the First World War . Film projections and moving sets animate the stories behind the artefacts, bringing them to life. The first section explores the building's heritage. On entering, a virtual admiral (copied from an actual painting of Michiel Adriaenszoon de Ruyter in the museum's collection) is shown pacing the room while real windows overlooking Amsterdam's harbour give glimpses of historical boats on the water. The second room contains a 360-degree projection of stormy seas overlaid with a montage of 400 years of Dutch naval history, including excerpts from the 18th-century sailor's letters. The third room was designed to convey the nightmarish scenario of the small girl rescued in her blanket from a sinking cruise liner after it was hit in the First World War. As with James Gardner's projects before them, the prevailing philosophy is that technology should serve the story rather than be a gimmick in and of itself.

In Asia, to celebrate Singapore's 200 years of existence since its founding in 1819, MET produced the fully immersive Bicentennial Experience. This timed walkthrough experience was presented in five "acts" – Beginnings, Arrival, Connectivity, Occupation and Destiny (including an indoor rainstorm). Embodying a distinct vein in MET's work of melding museum-like intellectual rigour into visceral experiences rather than simply didactic exhibitions, it received a 97 per cent approval rating from its 700,000 visitors.

Back in the UK, whereas "From Singapore to Singaporeans" was intended to elicit emotional responses of pride and belonging, BLINK aimed to inspire empathy. Working with Sightsavers, MET's challenge was to give a sense to the general public of the devastating of effects of trachoma, where sufferers gradually blink themselves blind. To convey this to visitors, they created the BLINK exhibition at the OXO Gallery which commissioned five award-winning photographers (Nick Knight, David Goldblatt, Kate Holt, Georgina Cranston and Tommy Trenchard) to create an image of something they would like to see before they went blind. An interactive interface was then developed by Jason Bruges Studio that used a tracking camera to capture the blink of each visitor. The technology gradually eroded each photograph leaving pictures abstractly distorted until the images were destroyed. The original artwork had already been destroyed and so the image was, rather poignantly, lost forever. This exposed each visitor to an emotional dimension

Figure 9.3 In Singapore's Bicentennial Experience visitors enjoyed an indoor tropical rainstorm
Source: Photograph by MET Studio.

in what would otherwise have been a formal exhibition experience and earned the project a Red Dot design award in 2020.

Box 9.1 Case study 9: Mobility Pavilion, Dubai Expo 2020

Expo projects are opportunities for designers to bring out all the tools in the interpretive and experiential box. MET Studio had previously produced two well-received Expo pavilions for Macau (Lisbon, 1998) and the Netherlands (Hannover, 2000). For the latter, they worked closely with the Dutch-government-appointed content developers and leading Dutch architects MVRDV to use slices of conceptual landscapes layered on top of each other to represent the themes of space and environment in one of the world's most crowded countries, showing how Holland uses technology and ecology to find living solutions for its citizens. This resulted in a series of startling spaces such as one shaped by the bottom of flowerpots and real, fully grown trees on the third floor.

A continuation of this impulse to inspire through spatial experiences was the Mobility Pavilion at Dubai's Expo 2020 (actually opened in October 2021 due to COVID-19 delays). The shell of the Mobility Pavilion, named Alif (after the first letter of the Arabic alphabet symbolising progress and new beginnings) was designed by Foster+Partners. With highly reflective, stainless-steel cladding inspired by chrome fenders and aircraft wings, its ribbed and curved shape evokes movement. Working within this fluid structure, the display areas are divided into three zones, each forming a petal in the tri-foil plan. Visitors enter the central core, which features the world's largest passenger lift capable of holding more than 160 persons which takes everyone up to the third level. From here, they can then move down through successive interconnected galleries to the lower ground floor, engaging with innovative, immersive and interactive experiences along the way.

Working closely with the client Expo 2020 Dubai, Ben Grossman (Magnopus) from LA and Weta from New Zealand, the storyline for the walkthrough immersive spaces was devised to represent the past, present and future of movement through the spirit of mobility rather than modes of transport *per se*. Each of the three zones had very different aesthetics and interpretive techniques, with highlights being Weta Workshop's 9-metre-tall, hyper-realistic representations of three major Arabic scholars of ancient navigation gathered around a giant, animated cartographer's table and an almost holographic show focusing on the hopes and dreams of a Bedouin girl.

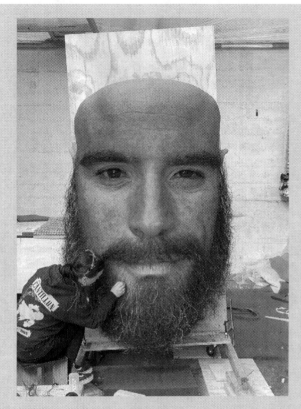

Figure 9.4 Production on one of Weta Workshop's hyper-realistic giants
for the Mobility Pavilion, Dubai Expo 2020
Source: Photograph by MET Studio.

According to MET's Creative Director, Peter Karn:

> Working very closely with the Expo 2020 team we set the bar incredibly high and set out to create a fully immersive, theatrical and cinematic story that visitors can physically walkthrough. We could not rely on post-production or virtual reality to create immersion due to the huge visitor numbers – we had to physically create the story in real-time. Technology allowed us to create more complex and ambitious concepts in a far more collaborative way than ever before. We quickly and efficiently tested solutions and proposals both from a visual and functional perspective without relying on physical fabrication. Technologies

Figure 9.5 An almost holographic show focused on the hopes and dreams of a Bedouin girl at the Mobility Pavilion, Dubai Expo 2020
Source: Photograph by MET Studio.

such as mixed and virtual reality allowed us to test our concepts in real-time and even create them as full virtual experiences. These processes also allowed for a far deeper collaborative process between the multiple disciplines and across the various regions all the collaborators were based in. Architecture, experiential design, audiovisuals, technical and interactive design were all aligned through digital processes allowing far more efficient results.

The Mobility Pavilion represents a high point to date of McCuaig's approach to creating experiences to inspire.

Conclusion

Museums are now recognised as having a multi-layered mission to care for collections, to communicate with a range of audiences and communities and to provide social spaces for raising awareness and activism. This evolution has been evolving over the 40 years of MET Studio's existence, and museum design companies have been judged by their ability to adapt to these changing circumstances. Alex McCuaig is a direct link to the post-war radicalism of James Gardner which sees exhibitions as places for the demystification of complex subject matter and the democratisation of information, diverging from the previously elitist and rarefied atmosphere of museum institutions. McCuaig believes that the public sector of museums and the private sector of design now have enough experience of each other's cultures to produce consistently excellent results catering for all ages and levels of interest worldwide. However, there will always be that (often healthy) tension between the publicly accountable museum and designers who want to take risks to push the boundary of what is possible and expected. At the heart of all McCuaig's projects, like his mentor James Gardner before him, has been an acknowledgement that museums are not meant to be encyclopaedic (redundant in the age of Wikipedia anyway), and that the role of the museum designer is primarily to create social experiences that inspire people to find out more: experiencing to inspire.

References

Cheung, S. (2008). Wetland tourism in Hong Kong: from birdwatcher to mass ecotourist. In Cochrane, J. *Asian tourism: growth and change.* Oxford; Amsterdam: Elsevier.

Ferris, M. (2000). Wired worlds. *Leonardo*, 33(2), 85–86.

Gardner, J. (1993). *The ARTful designer.* London: Centurion Press.

Pine, J. & Gilmore, J. (1999). *The experience economy: work is theatre & every business a stage.* Boston: Harvard Business School Press.

Conclusion

Understanding how museums have evolved in terms of their purpose, process and the people that influence them allows us to critically appraise the way museums are being developed for tourism today and into the future.

We have answered the question "What is heritage?" by defining it as history that can be or has been activated. When activated, heritage can bring a sense of pride and identity to a location, contributing to local, regional and national economies, but it can also be contentious. The re-evaluation of colonial and slave-related statues and monuments in the UK and US following the activism of the BLM movement points to this. And one of the best examples of this tension between authorised history and people's sense of heritage is the fate of Edward Colston's statue in Bristol, England. Having been unceremoniously ditched into the River Avon by protesters, the deposed, red-paint-daubed statue now lies in a Bristol museum, contextualised by the story of Colston's fortune making through slavery and the objections to memorialising him.

Tourism is as old as human civilisation. The notion of activated history (heritage) has been applied through the heritage tourism sector for thousands of years. It is a global phenomenon with provable roots as far back as the mid-second millennium BCE and heritage tourism is now a major economic force worldwide. The study of tourism, however, did not begin until the late 20th century, but it has given us an insight into what an intrinsically human activity it is, how heritage tourism products have developed and evolved and what a key industry it is in the world economy. Indeed, events such as pandemics reveal how reliant our economies are on cultural and heritage tourism.

Museums have mutated from simple repositories of objects to city-defining and, in some cases, nation-defining tourism attractions. In doing so, they have become flagships for regenerating whole cities and even countries. This has led to the diversification of museums, including how they address their audiences, how they are developed and expectations as

DOI: 10.4324/9781003369240-14

to how they will contribute to local, regional and national economies. Museums are now recognised as having a multi-layered mission of care for collections, the imperative to communicate with a range of audiences and communities and providing social spaces for raising awareness and activism. The level of development and understanding of the museum's role as a tourist attraction is not globally uniform and presents opportunities for government advisors and commercial consultants to get involved, positively contributing to economies, cultural enrichment and new experiences for visitors.

However, a growing number of people who may never have considered a career in the museum field are also finding themselves drawn into museum-like projects, whether that be within corporate environments or locally for tourism. Creating successful museum-like tourism attractions is largely a matter of how compellingly we tell relevant stories. Consequently, story-telling is at the heart of any museum or heritage experience development process. Interpretation or interpretive planning is the means by which the story is translated into design and key to this process is understanding the intended audience(s) of the heritage tourism product. Interpretation should create a sense of understanding, revelation, appreciation and even inspiration. It can be a call to action, to protect or conserve a habitat, cultural tradition or built environment. Creating a sense of place or identity is another potential way in which interpretation can contribute to tourism projects. It is important that storytelling does not get lost amongst the many other facets of large capital projects and ways of guarding against this include appreciating the value of interpretation and purposefully embedding it within the structure of the development and management processes for cultural and heritage tourism projects.

Museum design is complex and multidisciplinary and, as process, itself has been developing over the last 30–40 years. Consistency and efficacy in terms of project planning and management have greatly improved. The RIBA stages have been adapted over many years to aid in museum planning and design – from Feasibility (Stage 0) to Defects (Stage 6). Many lessons of best practice have been learned over this period but are easily forgotten in the fog of war that can be a new project. To ensure that a project continues to move forward, the client needs to establish a knowledgeable working group with a senior project champion who can take decisions and defend them to upper management. Within the consultant's team, the specialist skills required will vary from project to project. And to ensure that the resulting heritage tourism product is appropriately representative of the communities it serves, consultation with these communities needs to be built into the development process and preferably into the decision-making project structure itself.

The arrival of COVID-19 in 2020 was a major challenge to the tourist industry and by extension the museum world. Remote working was found to suit some forms of curatorship activity but it is hard to conduct collection or site conservation and security under such limiting circumstances. The museum's mission to provide public access to collections can be partly fulfilled by an enhanced online presence but often this means that larger, well-funded institutions just grab an even bigger share of the attention. The lifting of physical visitation restrictions requires first that institutions ensure their staff are confident, able and willing to return to work, as well as being well-trained in new preventative public health measures. In future, when physical visitation becomes a problem, there need to be new benchmarks for success of an attraction other than pure visitor numbers. There is still considerable scope for innovating in relation to how museums interact with their audiences in an age of pandemics.

The design world is full of influential and colourful characters. Museum design as a specialist creative discipline dealing with high-level concepts, architectural spaces and cutting-edge technology could be said to attract more than its fair share. Moreover, the polymathic nature of museum design seems to attract correspondingly wide-ranging intellects. John Ruskin (1819–1900) certainly fitted that bill, with interests spanning art, architecture, nature, tourism and the spiritual well-being of non-elitist audiences. He recognised the value in connecting us with authentic representations of the past, as well as creating aesthetically meaningful spaces within which to engage with museum and touristic experiences. To this end, Ruskin took practical steps to foster an awareness and practice of art for the general public through the creation of a drawing school and museums. One can say that he was one of the world's foremost advocates of "learning to look".

James Gardner, designer of the QE2 ocean liner, an important creative influence behind the 1951 Festival of Britain and founder of one of the world's most successful early museum-design companies, should really be a household name in the UK. He almost single-handedly established museum design as a burgeoning creative sector globally. He was a pioneer of narrative design for more than half a century. However, despite being one of Britain's most prolific and influential post-war designers, he is little known outside of academia. Gardner had an almost Ruskinesque faith in the general public's innate sense of curiosity; once he had piqued a visitor's interest he could lead them on a journey of discovery through his exhibition galleries. Key to arousing this sense of curiosity was his extensive and innovative use of interactive exhibits, in other words "interacting to learn".

With the museum-design sector taking off in earnest over the past 40 years, particularly in the UK and the US, the history of commercial museum-design companies themselves has become the subject of collection and research at universities such as Leicester and Brighton. Alex McCuaig is a direct link to the post-war radicalism of James Gardner which sees exhibitions as places for the demystification of complex subject matter and the democratisation of information, diverging from the previously elitist and rarefied atmosphere of museum institutions. McCuaig believes that the public sector of museums and the private sector of design now have enough experience of each other's cultures to produce consistently excellent results catering for all ages and levels of interest worldwide. At the heart of all McCuaig's projects, like his mentor James Gardner before him, has been an acknowledgement that museums are not meant to be encyclopaedic and that the role of the museum designer is primarily to create social experiences that inspire people to find out more.

It is my hope that this book serves a similar purpose.

Index

Printed in the United States
by Baker & Taylor Publisher Services